RENEWING

SALMON NATION'S

FOOD TRADITIONS

A RAFT list of food species and heirloom varieties

WITH TRADITIONS AT RISK AND IN NEED OF RECOVERY IN THE GREATER PACIFIC NORTHWEST

Compiled & edited by: GARY PAUL NABHAN

with: Ashley Rood, John Grahame, Laurie Monti

of the Center for Sustainable Environments at Northern Arizona University

Results of a workshop including: chefs, farmers, fisherfolk, food historians, orchardists, ethnobotanists, conservation activists, and nutrition educators

Contributors:

Nancy Turner, Sinclair Philip, Gerry Warren, Jennifer Hall, Debra Sohm Lawson, Makalé Faber, Elizabeth Woody, Fernando Divina, John Kallas, Eric Jones, Paul Atkinson, Peter de Garmo, Anthony Boutard, John Navazio, Coll Thrush, Joe McGarry, Dennis Martinez, Lora Lea Misterly, Kären Jurgensen, and Gary Paul Nabhan

PUBLISHED BY

RENEWING AMERICA'S FOOD TRADITIONS (RAFT) CONSORTIUM

IN COLLABORATION WITH

ECOTRUST

ecotrust

**Renewing America's
Food Traditions**

721 NW Ninth Ave., Suite 200
Portland, OR 97209
www.ecotrust.org

Ecotrust is a conservation
organization committed to
strengthening communities and
the environment from Alaska to
California. We work with native
peoples and in the fisheries,
forestry, and farming sectors
to build a regional economy
that is based on social and
ecological opportunities.

NAU/CSE Box 5765
Flagstaff, AK 86011
www.environment.nau.edu

The Renewing America's
Food Traditions consortium
includes: the Center for
Sustainable Environments,
Slow Food USA, Chefs
Collaborative, American
Livestock Breeds Conservancy,
Cultural Conservancy,
Native Seeds/SEARCH, and
Seed Savers Exchange in
collaboration with many NGOs
and tribes.

Copyright © 2006 by Renewing America's Food Traditions
Printed in Portland, Oregon, USA
All rights reserved. Except of brief quotations in critical articles or reviews, no part of this book may be
reproduced in any manner without prior written permission from the publisher.

Cataloging-in-Publication Data is on file with the Library of Congress
ISBN 0-9779332-0-2

Salmon Nation Lands & Waters map by Ben Donaldson, Andrew Fuller, and Charles Steinback

RAFT Regional Map of North America's Place-based Food Traditions concept by Gary Paul Nabhan,
illustration by Ron Redsteer

Cover and book design by Andrew Fuller

Printed with soy-based inks on recycled paper by Dynagraphics in Portland, Oregon
Text: 80# New Leaf Opaque Text, 100% recycled fiber, 100% post-consumer. Cover: 80# Reincarnation
Matte Cover, 100% recycled fiber, 100% post-consumer

To order copies of this publication:
for individual orders
www.salmonnation.com/foodtraditions

for bulk orders
http://oregonstate.edu/dept/press

CONTENTS

NOTE

ON HOW WE HAVE RANKED THREATS TO TRADITIONAL FOODS

In this book, descriptions of the level of threat to each food species or variety are close to those used by The World Conservation Union (IUCN) but are modified to include domesticated plants according to a 2005 article by Karl Hammer and Korous Khoshbakht in *Genetic Resources and Crop Evolution*, "Toward a red list for crop plant species."

Our categories are as follows:

Extinct—(e.g. Steller's sea cow).

Extinct in the Landscape—Species or varieties are represented in conservation collections such as seed banks, botanical gardens, or zoos but are no longer in wild habitats, farmers' fields, or orchards (e.g. Marshall strawberry).

Endangered—Stocks or populations are legally protected or agriculturally vulnerable to loss in one or more states or nations (e.g. Chinook salmon).

Threatened—Use of stocks or populations may be legally or agriculturally limited in one or more states or nations (e.g. Pink salmon).

Biologically or Culturally at Risk—Stocks or populations are dependent on conservation actions to be culturally used and safely consumed (e.g. Licorice fern)—a level equivalent to the IUCN's "vulnerable" category.

Recovering—Species or populations that had once declined or been contaminated and are now increasing due to recent conservation actions (e.g. Inchelium red garlic).

Status Unknown—Let's get out in the field to discover what's really going on!

ECOTRUST ON
REVIVING FOOD TRADITIONS

Renewing Salmon Nation's Food Traditions describes a treasure trove of regional plants and animals—some at risk, others recovering. We hope that it can serve as both a reference guide and a historical inventory of species that were once abundant in Salmon Nation.

At the back, this handbook also features a resource guide—a listing of nurseries and seed companies serving the region. With this information in hand, it is up to us to bring these fruits, vegetables, herbs, and shellfish back into widespread cultivation. Farmers can help by growing these varieties, and chefs and retailers can join in by featuring them on restaurant menus and at grocery stores.

Wild-harvested species present a different case, because best practices for sustainable harvesting are often gear-specific or place-based. For salmon, we encourage readers to seek wild caught, not farmed, Pacific salmon. For other fish species, it is important to learn how the animal was caught. Those harvested by hook and line or pot caught are the most sustainably harvested. For mushrooms and berries, harvest methods are important as well. Mushrooms should be cut at the stem rather then plucked from the ground, with care taken not to erode the soil around them. Most berries should be picked individually from the plant, rather than raked. Care should be exercised not to intrude upon the traditional gathering grounds of indigenous peoples.

We have an opportunity to work together so that all this food diversity can become common once again. Please support the markets, restaurants, and roadside stands that already feature these foods. There is a role for each of us in re-establishing the viability of Salmon Nation's rich food traditions.

Debra Sohm Lawson

Director of Food and Farms
Market Connections, Ecotrust

SLOW FOOD USA ON
SAFEGUARDING AND HONORING THE
TRADITIONAL FOODS OF SALMON NATION

Both the idea for this book and the process of creating it capture the ambitions of the international Slow Food movement—to collaboratively recognize, document, celebrate, and preserve our food biodiversity. The group of passionate Pacific Northwesterners that built this list mirrors a dynamic core in each of the U.S. food nations. Commercial farmers, native land stewards, chefs, ethnobotanists, food retailers, and consumers used the list of foods from this rich agricultural region to acknowledge their connectedness and are now working together strategically to build a more virtuous food system. This list, which we hope is the first of many, raises the profile of socially and environmentally important foods. It can and should be used as a point of entry into safeguarding and honoring America's place-based heritage foods that feed our bodies, minds, and communities.

Makalé Faber

Slow Food USA Program Officer
for RAFT, Presidia, and the
Ark of Taste

CHEFS COLLABORATIVE ON
CELEBRATING THE DIVERSITY
OF LOCAL FOODS

Preserving foods with heritage, of diverse flavor and purpose, native to an area and its cultures, we draw upon the skills and passion of those willing to cross artificial boundaries between mainstream economics and our country's history of survival. The convening of this group and the resulting capture of information portends a wonderful convergence and opportunity for our food system and our communities. Chefs Collaborative has always celebrated and promoted the diversity and use of local foods. As the pace of life continues to accelerate, people have less time to create meals of their own. Restaurants often fill this niche, offering the satisfaction of relaxed conversation over a good meal, and delivering everything from a daily dinner to big-budget celebrations. Our members are honored to use their gathering places as a means to revitalize the history of our nation's food and culture, and do so with local relevance and impact.

Jennifer Hall

Executive Director,
Chefs Collaborative

INTRODUCTION

Salmon Nation's coastal rainforests, muskegs, mudflat clam beds, Palouse prairies, and river canyons look and feel unlike any other in the world. You can sense the distinctiveness of this eco-region wherever you travel within it—from Alaska, the Yukon Territory, British Columbia, Washington, Idaho, western Montana, Oregon, and northern California. But Salmon Nation also tastes unlike any other place—from its huckleberries and Oregon grapes to its Dungeness crab and alder-smoked salmon. Its indigenous and ethnic immigrant food traditions offer us altogether unique flavors, fragrances, textures, and colors to put on our plates. Great chefs and restauranteurs such as Angelo Pelligrini, Sinclair Philip, Greg Higgins, Adrian Beaty, Jonathan Sundstrom, Fernando Divina, and Kären Jurgensen have used the seafoods, fungi, berries, and vegetables unique to the region to create a deeply memorable cuisine.

The pleasures of Salmon Nation's unique foods, from ooligan grease to herring spawn, have enlivened the world-renowned potlatches, those ceremonial feasts held by the First Nations of the Pacific coast. You can pick up on the excitement over Salmon Nation's unique nutritional resources even in the journals of Lewis and Clark from two centuries ago. Their expedition was literally saved by their native companions' traditional ecological and culinary knowledge of what foods were available during the winter that they spent along the Columbia River. You can taste the landscape in the venison and the wheat nourishing H.L. Davis's *Honey in the Horn,* the first Pulitzer Prize–winning novel of the Pacific Northwest. It flavors Tlingit poet Nora Marks Dauenhauer's recipe for "How to Make Good Baked Salmon from the River," and other poems by Gary Snyder, Elizabeth Woody, Kim Stafford, and Dick Hugo. The pride of Salmon Nation artists for their food is evident in their colorful labels for canned wild-caught fish and crab, and in their posters and polo shirts proclaiming that "Friends don't let friends eat farmed salmon."

Among all the "food nations" of North America—ranging from Clambake Nation to Chile Pepper Nation—Salmon Nation is the richest in mushrooms, berries, wild roots, fish, and shellfish. Native American traditions are at its core, but Russian, Spanish, Scandinavian, Japanese, Filipino, African, and Basque have added other culinary accents to the mix.

Notwithstanding the historic richness and current interest in the culinary legacies of the Pacific Northwest, many of the plant and animal species upon which these legacies were originally based are now threatened, endangered, or contaminated with everything from mercury to pesticides to sea lice. Of nearly 180 species that formed the basis of food traditions in the Pacific Northwest for centuries, roughly three-quarters are now at risk biologically or culturally, or are listed as threatened, endangered, or extinct. One-third of them are legally threatened and endangered. The cornucopia that has fed residents of Salmon Nation since time immemorial is now being emptied. At this point in time, less than one-tenth of the traditional foods we surveyed are on their way to significant recovery.

Nevertheless, habitat restoration and species recovery efforts for selected food plants and animals have been remarkably successful within Salmon Nation. Grassroots conservation organizations and tribes have restored salmon streams, camas wetlands, berry patches, and degraded farmlands. These restoration efforts are much in the spirit of Slow Food's "Presidia" projects, which form a stronghold within which heritage foods can be safeguarded and revitalized. We do not believe that every plant or animal species formerly used as food in Salmon Nation should be targeted for future commercial sales and consumption; some, like the abalone, seals, and sturgeon, may take decades before they biologically recover to former population levels, and even then their human consumption may not necessarily be recommended. However, we do believe that "eco-gastronomists" should support the habitat restoration and population recovery for all of the species listed here, even if we are never to taste some of them again. They are part of our continent's cultural, culinary, or in some cases, agricultural heritage. We should not forget what has nourished our ancestors in the past; culinary Alzheimer's is not a disease that will help shape a more humane and healthful future for ourselves and other creatures on this planet.

The following RAFT list is an attempt to prevent such a disease from overtaking us and our food choices. Nearly every one of these species deserves more recognition, documentation, and celebration, regardless of whether or not they are promoted as "future foods" per se. We encourage all readers and eaters in Salmon Nation to familiarize themselves with the rich histories, ecologies, and recipes of these 170-some food species, and to honor their original stewards.

We are grateful to those who have contributed to this initial list, and welcome commentaries from you about other foods we may have inadvertently neglected to include here.

Gary Paul Nabhan, Ph.D.

Director, Center for Sustainable
Environments, RAFT founder

DOMESTICATED CROPS

CULTIVATED FRUITS AND NUTS

APPLE

Hudson's golden gem apple *(Malus X domestica)*. A large, conical, elongated russet with smooth skin and crisp, juicy, almost nutty flavor. This heirloom makes an excellent dessert apple and is a good keeper. It was discovered as a fencerow seedling in Tangent, Oregon in 1931 and promoted early on by Tangent's Hudson Nursery. Although sixteen nurseries still offer it, its former position as the most heralded russet in the Northwest has

Hudson's golden gem apple

been diminished. While the apple itself is not threatened, russet apple traditions in the Pacific Northwest are declining and at risk.

Orenco apple *(Malus X domestica)*. This is a medium to large apple with light dots mottling its bright red skin; its juicy white flesh is crisp and tender, with a mildly sweet, piquant flavor. It was introduced as a "the ideal dessert apple" by the Oregon Nursery Company in the town of Orenco in 1920, during its heyday as the largest nursery in the West. The Orenco apple's culinary qualities, such as aroma and taste, were considered so pleasing that it was compared favorably to the Doubler Red McIntosh and Spitzenberg, two other heirlooms that for decades set the standards for quality. However, the five nurseries that still offered it in 1988 had dwindled to three by 2000. Ripening in mid-September, this twentieth century standard is hardy and scab-resistant, but threatened in terms of its limited commercial availability.

Pacific crabapple or **Swamp crabapple** *(Malus fusca)*. With tiny, tart, cherrylike fruits good for jelly, this was formerly an important fruit for indigenous peoples of the West Coast. Moreover, this species is good as a rootstock, restoration shrub,

Pacific crabapple

or as wildlife habitat on swampy sites that are otherwise too wet for apples. It has a wide tolerance for cold but is commercially available only from Burnt Ride Nursery in Onalaska, Washington, and Forestfarm Nursery in Williams, Oregon. On the north coast of British Columbia, First Nations recognize several different varieties of the crabapple, varying in size, color, and taste. The status of these varieties is not currently known.

Spokane beauty apple *(Malus X domestica)*. This historic variety was hailed as the "largest apple known, a prodigy for size; of extraordinary beauty...; flesh crisp, juicy, rich with a delicious, high flavor. Unsurpassed for cooking and drying; a very long keeper...." The origins of this heirloom go back to 1859, when a Stephen Mason, Sr. carried a bag of apple seeds with him westward on the Oregon Trail. After he settled near Walla Walla, he planted the seeds and selected one sport that grew into a tree producing particularly large apples weighing over two pounds. Although the apples are good for drying, cooking, or eating fresh, the variety fell from commercial use because of the large, unwieldy, irregularly shaped fruit. It is now available only from six nurseries, and can be considered threatened in the landscape.

Northwestern greenling apple *(Malus X domestica)*. A large, handsome apple with pale-green waxy skin that turns yellow after maturing, this is a popular winter-keeping variety that originated in Wisconsin around 1872 and was then adapted to the Northwest. It remains available from fifteen nurseries, so is not at risk but may be declining in commerce.

APRICOT

Blenheim apricot *(Prunus armeniaca)*. A medium-large fruit with red dots scattered across a pale orange skin, this freestone apricot has juicy aromatic flesh. A distinctive variety by 1830 in Great Britain, it became famous in northern California for its canning and drying qualities. Setting the standard for sweet apricots for decades, this apricot remains available from thirteen nurseries—mostly in California, Washington, and Oregon—so is not considered at risk.

Wenatchee Moorpark apricot *(Prunus armeniaca)*. This yellow-skinned, large oval apricot is a heavy bearer with excellent flavor and is a longtime favorite in the Pacific Northwest. It was among the first introductions (1908) of the C&O Nursery of Wenatchee, Washington, which was founded in 1906 and remains open a century later. Seven other nurseries offer its stock, so it is not at risk but is regionally restricted.

BLACKBERRY AND BERRY HYBRID

Loganberry *(Rubus ursinus* var. *loganobaccus).* Thought to be an accidental cross between a wild dewberry *(Rubus ursinus)* and an old variety of red raspberry *(Rubus idaeus),* this thornless shrub has large, light red berries that darken as they ripen. After being selected by Judge J. H. Logan in Santa Cruz, California, in 1881, its introduction into trade became a landmark in the history of small fruits. Many Pacific Northwesterners prefer its flavor above all other cultivated berries. It was also a favorite for wine making in the early to mid-1900s. Although its acreage in the Pacific Northwest exceeded four thousand acres by 1919, there are less than one hundred acres of commercial plantings left in the region. Still offered to home gardeners by ten nurseries, it is threatened.

Olympic blackberry *(Rubus ursinus X R. leucodermis).* Not unlike the cascadeberry and tayberry, this is an *ursinus*-derived hybrid. In this case, the Olympic is a hybrid between Luther Burbank's "phenomenal" blackberry and a blackcap raspberry *(Rubus leucodermis),* with fruit nearly two inches long, juicy and sweet with a memorable flavor. The Olympic originated on Vashon Island, where it was developed in the late 1920s by Peter Erickson and his son-in-law, H. F. Grieder. It became an immediate rage in Seattle, sold at farmers' markets and

Olympic blackberry

even at the famous department store, Frederick & Nelson's. For a number of years, the Olympic was celebrated by those who toured the region on the train route called "The Big Berry," but as berry production by the Erickson and Grieder families ebbed, so did the popularity of this heirloom. Only a few growers keep this berry alive today, but they remain devoted to it and its exceptional flavor. Threatened.

CHERRY

Black Republican cherry *(Prunus avium).* Long considered one of the greater sweet cherries of the West, the Black Republican has medium to large, dark-red fruit that turn almost pitch black at maturity. They are sweet, distinctively flavored, and of excellent keeping quality. Seth Lewelling was the observant nurseryman who found this cherry at Milwaukie, Oregon and selected one chance seedling that appeared in a row of several common cherry varieties. It became commercially available in 1860, and for the following seven decades, it was praised for the flavor of its purplish red flesh: "Tender, meaty, crisp, mild, sweet…of good quality." The name was inspired by Lewelling's abolitionist political leanings just before the Civil War, for like him, a "Black Republican" opposed slavery. Today, the Black Republican has nearly disappeared, and is offered by only four nurseries. A few trees survive around Eugene, Oregon, including two of the largest, oldest cherry trees in Salmon Nation. It may be considered endangered in the landscape.

Bing cherry *(Prunus avium).*

Bing cherry

The same Seth Lewelling of Black Republican fame was also responsible for launching the career of this sweet cherry in Salmon Nation and beyond. Becoming the leading commercial cherry of the West, the Bing was named so by Lewelling to honor a Chinese foreman, Ah Sit Bing, who had worked for years at his Milwaukie nursery and who had cared for the trial plots in which the cherry was found. Not long after its introduction, it was described in *The Willamette Farmer* as "very dark throughout...very rich and solid...and will not bleed when the stem is removed from the fruit." It has since become the standard in texture, flavor, and size for sweet cherries, with its heart-shaped, purple freestone flesh that is firm

Family Food Traditions

As a child growing up in small-town Wisconsin, eating in the school lunchroom could sometimes be embarrassing. I'd look around to see my friends holding their Wonder Bread sandwiches and Twinkies, knowing that the contents of my lunch box were vastly different: a sandwich on inch-thick homemade bread and chocolate cake made from scratch. I'd cautiously pull out my sandwich, hoping they wouldn't notice.

Only later did I come to appreciate my mom's love of good food. I've discovered that her traditions fostered in me a deep sense of place. We grew our tomatoes organically in a small garden plot next to our back porch. We canned summer peaches from a local farm stand. And we made applesauce from apples that we picked at an orchard down the road.

Today, although rows of houses occupy the land where the farm stand and the apple orchard once were, my family's food traditions live on. Now living in Portland, Oregon, my husband and I grow a great diversity of vegetables and fruits, including fifteen varieties of tomatoes, a few varieties of beans, loganberries, and hood strawberries. In the fall, we gather and preserve wild huckleberries and mushrooms such as chanterelles, hedgehogs, and boletes. These foods sustain us year round. All thanks to my mom, who taught us how to grow and preserve food, and who passed on her love of cooking and of the family food traditions that are cultivated along the way.

Debra Sohm Lawson is a gardener and conservationist who serves as Ecotrust's Director of Food and Farms Market Connections.

and meaty. However, it is not very hardy in cooler climes, and is finicky about what other varieties it accepts as pollinators. Bing, like the lighter Rainier cherry, is certainly not at risk, since more than thirty nurseries continue to offer it, but its pie traditions may be in decline.

Lambert cherry *(Prunus avium).* Slightly smaller than the Bing, this is a dark red, heart-shaped cherry developed in Oregon around 1855, once again from a seedling found by Lewelling in a Milwaukie, Oregon, orchard belonging to J. H. Lambert. This time, however, Lewelling grafted scion from this promising selection onto a May Duke rootstock for extra hardiness. Then, in 1880, another chance occurrence took this stock in another direction: the crown of two-decade-old tree died and new growth with a mix of parental traits called "a bud sport" emerged from the roots. Described as "tender and melting, sprightly, pleasant flavored, tart; of very good quality," it became ranked second only to Bing in Salmon Nation and is still sold by twelve nurseries. While not at risk, it has been declining in trade over the last two decades.

CURRANT AND GOOSEBERRY

Oregon champion gooseberry *(Ribes divaricatum).* This cultivated coastal black gooseberry bush produces medium-large, yellowish green gooseberries that sweeten as they ripen, becoming better and better for wines, pies, and jams. Originating in Salem, Oregon, sometime before 1880, this gooseberry variety has remained prolific for more than two decades and hardy across several zones of climate in the Northwest. It is available from at least eight nurseries, and does not appear to be at risk.

FIG

Gillette fig *(Ficus carica).* A sweet, yellow fig fine for fresh eating, canning, or drying, the Gillette produces a single crop in July and early August. Grown commercially in Washington and Oregon in the 1930s, it is now available only from Oregon Exotics Rare Fruit Nursery in Grants Pass. Endangered.

Gillette fig

PEACH

Charlotte peach *(Prunus persica).* An old, rediscovered freestone variety, this large, tasty peach ripens in late August in Oregon. It is available only from One Green World, formerly Northwoods Retail Nursery, of Molalla, Oregon. Endangered.

Charlotte peach

PEAR

Orcas pear *(Pyrus communis).* A large yellow pear with a carmine blush, this versatile fruit is well-suited to fresh eating, home canning, or drying; its core seldom breaks down as it ripens, making it ideal for small-scale processing. It was discovered by Joe Long on Orcas Island, Washington, decades ago. The trees have a vigorous open spreading habit, suitable for home orchards. Because it is available from only four nurseries in Washington and Oregon, its long-term survival should be considered threatened.

Orcas pear

STRAWBERRY

Hood strawberry *(Fragaria X ananassa).* A large, glossy red berry that glistens as it ripens, it is excellent for home jam and jelly making. It was named for the Hood River, where several varieties were pioneered in the Pacific Northwest. Although still a popular home garden variety, only five nurseries, all in the Northwest, still offered it by 2000, compared to eight in 1998. Declining, and threatened.

Marshall strawberry *(Fragaria X ananassa).* With rich, dark-red flesh to its very center, the Marshall strawberry was once considered the finest eating berry on the continent by virtue of its juicy, aromatic, and pleasantly sprightly flavor. A chance seedling was discovered in the Northeast in 1890, but over the following six decades it found its most productive home in Washington, Oregon, and northern California, where it was the backbone of the frozen berry industry. It all but vanished after World War II because it was too delicate to ship fresh, and is no longer available from any commercial nursery. Extinct in the landscape.

WALNUT

Spurgeon special walnut *(Juglans regia).* This Persian or English walnut flowers relatively late compared to other heirloom nuts, thereby avoiding frosts and offering yields that are larger than most. Its nuts are of average size but have a delicate, agreeable flavor. This heirloom was selected by John R. Spurgeon, an early settler of Clark County, who then spent the next four decades trying to drum up interest in his favorite selection. When the Oregon-Washington Nut Growers Association finally recognized the value of his variety, Spurgeon had already retired, so a colleague named J. B. Bruce took over promoting the Spurgeon for several more decades. As the Spurgeon trees age, they become more and more reliable as producers of fair to good yields, which can be enhanced by planting Franquette walnut trees nearby as pollinators. However, only three nurseries now carry this heirloom, so it can be considered endangered.

HEIRLOOM VEGETABLES

BEAN

Gramma Walters bean *(Phaseolus vulgaris).* This is a spectacularly mottled, very colorful pole bean, an heirloom that has its roots in eastern Washington. Gramma Walters has both speckled pods and seed, the latter of the well-known cranberry horticultural bean type. Gramma Walters is early-maturing, thereby avoiding damage by most frosts, making it a reliable producer in the cooler climes of Salmon Nation. Used primarily as a dry bean, it loses some of its vibrant maroon hues after boiling. Experts are not sure who Gramma Walters was, or when she developed these beans. An early favorite heirloom offered by Abundant Life Seeds, it has declined in availability but still may be found in gardens of seed savers.

Immigrant bean *(Phaseolus vulgaris)*. An heirloom variant of dark-red kidneys that is well-adapted to southern Oregon. This bush bean produces small golden yellow seeds. Only one U.S. and two Canadian seed outlets continue to offer it. Endangered.

Kilham goose bean *(Phaseolus vulgaris)*. A bush bean with shiny, purple-on-white round seeds, this heirloom was kept alive for years by the Kilham family of Port Townsend, Washington. It is now offered occasionally by just two seed companies, including Abundant Life Seeds. Endangered.

Lucas navy bean *(Phaseolus vulgaris)*. The dry pea bean has small white seeds that mature relatively early in the Pacific Northwest. This heirloom from the Puget Sound area has been available for the last two decades only through Abundant Life Seeds, which does not currently list it. Endangered.

Nez Perce bean *(Phaseolus vulgaris)*. Kin to the dry heirloom bean historically called Squaw Yellow, this half-climber has small, yellow-tan seeds with a rich flavor for soups. Derived from the Nez Perce culture in the 1930s, it was maintained for decades by the Denny family in Idaho. Available from one Canadian and two U.S. seed outlets. Endangered.

Oregon giant bean *(Phaseolus vulgaris)*. This pole-climbing bean has tender, mottled, giant pods with excellent flavor and nearly stringless texture. The foot-long, curving pods serve as a sweet and tender green bean when immature, but they can also be dried when mature and threshed to produce a dry bean for boiling or baking. The Oregon giant is climatically adapted to Salmon Nation's coooler, cloudier coastal zones, and does well on the cold soils of mountain ranges there as well. This heirloom was first described in the region early in the last century, with the Portland Seed Co. offering it as Dickenson's Yount in 1921. Today, this old-time bean is offered by only five seed companies: one in Canada, one in Washington, one in California, and two in Montana. It has largely disappeared from markets and is now endangered.

Oregon giant bean

Paint bean *(Phaseolus vulgaris)*. Originally a sport from a yellow-eye dry soup bean, this bean has yellow eye rings on a white background. It is a drought-adapted, early maturing bush bean from eastern Washington that is now offered only by Prairie Garden Seeds in Saskatchewan. Endangered.

Whatcom (lima) half runner bean *(Phaseolus vulgaris).* This pole bean has very large white seeds that look like limas. It is a variant on another Oregon half-runner. No longer offered commercially, it is endangered.

CORN

Hooker's Sweet Indian corn

Hooker's Sweet Indian corn *(Zea mays).* This sweet corn from Olympia, Washington, is white when young but matures to blue-black on thin, five to seven inch ears. It was adapted to the Pacific Northwest through five decades of selection by Ira Hooker, an Olympia area resident. It is now offered by only five companies, three of them in the Northwest. Threatened.

MELON

Oregon delicious melon *(Cucumis melo).* An early-maturing but large melon with orange flesh and outstanding flavor, this football-shaped muskmelon is well-adapted to the maritime climate of the Pacific slopes of the Cascades. It is considered endangered by Seeds of Diversity, with just two commercial sources, and a few backyard growers. Endangered.

ONION AND GARLIC

Inchelium red garlic

Inchelium red garlic *(Allium sativum* var. *sativum).* This garlic has very large artichoke-type bulbs with purple blotching on white or yellowish skin and is faint purple at the base. Stores six to nine months and has a true mild garlic flavor. It was discovered on the Colville Indian Reservation, but its early history is obscure. Recovering.

Lorz Italian garlic

Lorz Italian garlic *(Allium sativum* var. *sativum).* This heirloom garlic was brought to Washington's Columbia basin from Italy by the Lorz family before 1900. It is artichoke-like with large, very flat, round bulbs. Its flavor varies from year to year—ranging from medium-warm to hot—and lingers on the palate. Recovering.

Nootka rose garlic *(Allium sativum* var. *sativum).* This heirloom garlic is from the San Juan Islands, off the northern coast of mainland Washington. It has a medium to large bulb, streaked red on mahogany. Its cloves often have a long paper trail that are very attractive for braiding when one or two bulb wrappers are removed to show the bright-red clove tips. Its flavor is medium to strong and very good for raw eating. Recovering.

POTATO

Dimick potato *(Solanum tuberosum)*. Among the most poorly known of all American spuds, this heirloom dates back to the heyday of the Oregon Trail in the mid-nineteenth century. When pioneer A. R. Dimick came west on the trail to Salmon Nation, he brought potato starts with him that he later planted in Marion County, Oregon. His contemporaries described it as the best-tasting potato to ever grow in their parts, but today it may be altogether extinct in cultural landscapes.

Ozette potato *(Solanum tuberosum)*. This historic oblong fingerling potato was said to have been brought from Peru in the late 1700s by Spanish explorers who planted it at Neah Bay, Washington, and on Vancouver Island before abandoning their forts within a year's time. The Ozette, as well as the more obscure To-le-ak and Haida potatoes are unlike any others now in North America, since all other varieties went through a bottleneck in Europe before crossing seas back to North America. Even though the Spanish departed, their potatoes persisted and were adopted by the Makah living

Ozette potato

at Ozette village. Classic in appearance with pale beige-pink skin and creamy, almost waxy yellow flesh, the Ozette's slightly nutty, earthy flavor comes through beautifully when lightly steamed or sautéed. It has been found in Makah dooryard gardens for so long that they are considered a native traditional food. It has been honored on the Ark of Taste, and is recovering.

Pride of Multnomah potato *(Solanum tuberosum)*. Record-setting in terms of its yields of up to 790 bushels per acre, this heirloom spud was introduced in 1909 by the Portland Seed Company, and rapidly gained fame in Salmon Nation. In the Portland Seed Company's 1921 catalog, the Pride of Multnomah was described as "of the ideal elongated type with smooth, thin white skin, eyes shallow; flesh snow white, of finest table quality; flowers white, vines medium large of bushy growth, withstands drought; and is blight and disease resistant to a remarkable degree." Although first rooted in Washington and Oregon, Pride of Multnomah set the early twentieth century yield record in California, generating 790 bushels on a single acre plot near the Panama Pacific Exposition in 1915. It has since fallen from grace and from commercial distribution. Its status in the landscape is unknown.

SQUASH

Lower Salmon River squash *(Cucurbita maxima)*. This large turban squash weighs up to ten pounds and has a pale, pinkish orange color. It grows on long vines that are well adapted to the interior of the Pacific Northwest. Endangered.

SEA FOODS

ECHINODERMS

California sea cucumber *(Parastichopus californicus)*. A globally widespread, colorful, and highly commercial sea cucumber, this species prefers bedrock tidepools and eelgrass beds off Vancouver Island. It was historically used there but began to be harvested commercially around 1980. However, several areas on the coast of Salmon Nation are now closed to fishing, and the sea cucumber remains vulnerable to overharvesting.

Sea urchin *(Strongylocentrotus* species). Red, green, and purple sea urchin species support a commercial fishery that often exceeds eighty million dollars in export sales from California alone. Commercially marketed, the purple urchin is especially popular in the Pacific Northwest. Alaskan Tlingit and Tsimshian clans "owned" certain sea urchin beds for harvesting. Both the roe and the raw urchin have been consumed by resident peoples, but these traditions are now in decline due to export of most harvested urchins to Asia. Traditions are at risk.

Sea urchin

FISH

COD AND HAKE

Pacific cod *(Gadus microcarpa* or *Gadus macrocephala)*. A silvery gray or brown fish with three dorsal fins, Pacific cod run in schools above gravelly and rocky bottoms forty feet deep or more, from southeast Alaska to northern California. Their schools are commonly trawled, but severe declines observed between 1994 and 1996 caused the Canadian government to place strict vessel quotas in order to maintain populations. Once common, stocks are now in decline, except in parts of Alaska. Although not biologically threatened, cultural traditions are at risk.

Pacific hake *(Merluccius productus)*. A gray fish with two dorsal fins, Pacific hake reaches three feet in length under optimal conditions. Known for its soft flakey texture and codlike taste, it remains firm when fried or sautéed and keeps relatively intact in stews, soups, and casseroles. Within the last decade, fish stick and surimi industries, for which Pacific hake is a principal resource, have developed on the west coast of Oregon and Vancouver Island, British Columbia. Pacific hake is rapidly being overexploited and is threatened.

GREENLING

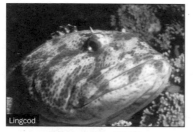

Lingcod

Lingcod *(Ophiodon elongatus)*. This particular greenling is a long-lived bottomfish taken by scuba-diving sportsmen and commercial fishermen, including those from several First Nation cultures. There are a few populations landlocked in freshwater lakes. The flesh is tasty and turns white when cooked. Populations of various lingcod stocks are currently just a fraction of what they were one hundred years ago, and in some places, the U.S. government has ordered drastic reductions in allowable takes. Sports fishery harvests are currently often competitive with commercial harvests. Recent local stock recoveries may be undermined if growing pressures are not arrested.

HERRING

Pacific herring *(Clupea pallasi)*. Spawn harvesting and herring raking are ancient traditions in Alaska, Canada, and the Pacific Northwest, where they are still practiced in early spring along the shores of many bays and coves. The spawn is a delicacy harvested from kelp ribbons, spruce, fir, or cedar boughs placed in the water. However, Pacific herring roe has also become a delicacy for sushi lovers, for whom the roe is destructively harvested straight from the belly of the female herring. Over 90 percent of the Pacific herring now caught is for the roe or eggs inside the herring. As Hilary Stewart wrote, "Today fishermen complain that herring runs are depleted by over fishing [but] Indians once went out in canoes to meet herring that schooled in uncountable numbers." Pacific herring themselves remain overfished in certain localities, despite state policies to regulate harvests to leave enough for wildlife. The spawn-on-kelp fishery is currently limited to specific spawning stocks in northern Puget Sound, British Columbia, and southeastern Alaska. Traditions are at risk and rapidly declining.

LAMPREY

Pacific or **Trident lamprey** *(Lampetra tridentata).* One of four lampreys of Northwestern rivers and bays that has suffered severe declines, this one was also widely harvested for food by Native Americans in centuries past. Formerly occurring from northern California through the Columbia River, lampreys were so abundant that they literally cloaked the Willamette Falls in the 1880s. More recently, counts of Snake River populations have declined from fifty thousand in the 1960s to less than one thousand in the 1990s. The lamprey's commercial harvest is all but over, though First Nations are struggling to maintain their traditional rights to this food source. It is endangered as a traditional food.

ROCKFISH

Pacific rockfish *(Sebastes* spp.). The Pacific rockfishes are heavy bodied, big-lipped fish that often travel in dense schools and rest at night on the subtidal bottom. They formerly comprised the core of the U.S. bottom fish harvest on the Pacific coast, but most rockfishes are now threatened by overexploitation. More than thirty species found off the California, Oregon, and Washington coasts may be in decline. The sustainability of each fishery is dependent upon the kind of fishing gear that is primarily used in a particular fishing ground. Some of these species are often inadvertently caught as bycatch and killed by trawlers seeking other kinds of fish. Rockfish species are sometimes sold as "Pacific snapper." Most rockfish populations on the West Coast have experienced such dramatic declines in their abundance that governments are limiting allowable takes in areas where they can be targeted.

Bocaccio *(Sebastes paucispinis).* Formerly an important species in commercial fisheries from northern California through Canada, this is the largest rockfish in the Pacific. It dwells amid the rocky reefs where it is overharvested by trawlers. Populations of bocaccio have been severely depleted by a combination of trawling and resulting disruption of bottom habitat, and by changing oceanographic conditions. The life history characteristics of

Bocaccio

bocaccio—late maturation, extreme longevity (with lifespans formerly up to two hundred years), and allegiance to spawning sites—make these fish particularly vulnerable. The U.S. government has considered bocaccio stocks to be overfished enough to mandate drastic reductions in allowable takes. Canada has listed it as threatened after declines of over 90 percent off Vancouver Island between 1980 and 2000. Endangered as a cultural tradition.

China rockfish *(Sebastes nebulosus)*. Like other rockfishes, this yellow-speckled black fish was formerly common from Alaska to California in rocky inshore areas along exposed coastlines. Its numbers have declined in many places along the Pacific Northwest coast. Threatened.

Shortspine thornyhead rockfish *(Sebastolobus alascanus)*. This red or pink bottom-feeder is rare in shallow waters from the Bering Sea to Baja California but may be common in deeper, open seas. Because it remains still when seen by spearfishing scuba divers, it has earned the name "idiot fish," and its nearshore populations may be vulnerable. Its habitats are being disrupted by trawling and dredging. At risk for culinary use.

Widow rockfish *(Sebastes entomelas)*. This commonly fished sculpin ranges from Kodiak Island, Alaska, down to Baja California. Its brassy brown body is compressed sideways, reaching a maximum size of just over twenty inches in length and four pounds in weight. Feeding on small crabs, squid, and anchovies, this is a fish of deep rocky environments that is susceptible to disturbance by trawling and dredging. Among sports fishermen, it is one of the most sought after of fifty-some rockfish managed and regulated in California, Oregon, Washington, and British Columbia. When they form huge schools in midwater depths, widow rockfish become extremely vulnerable to sports fishermen as well as commercial trawling gear and are often taken in great quantities.

Yelloweye rockfish

Yelloweye or **Red rockfish** *(Sebastes ruberrimus)*. This red to yellow solitary fish has prominent spines between its nape, and reaches a maximum of three feet in length. All young are red, and seek shelter in the hollows of sponges or in crags around rocky offshore reefs. These red rockfish may be declining due to habitat disruption by trawlers but are not so negatively impacted by hook and line fishermen. At risk for culinary use.

Yellowtail rockfish *(Sebastes flavidus)*. This gray or green-brown fish has a yellow-green tail and fins, yellow streaks behind its eyes, and formerly reached over two feet in length. Its typically encountered sizes and numbers have declined so much that it is rarely sold by those who catch it and hardly seen in the fish markets of the Pacific Northwest anymore. Its numbers are declining, so it is increasingly rare in trade. At risk for culinary use.

SABLEFISH

Pacific black or **Alaska cod, Sablefish,** or **Butterfish** *(Anoplopoma fimbria).* This species is neither a true cod nor a butterfish. Its high fat content makes it an excellent fish for smoking, after which it is commonly marketed as smoked black cod. Foreign demand, particularly from Japan, takes most of the catch. Combined with pressures from domestic use, seasonal limitations have had to be set on what was once a year-round fishery. Several major stocks of this sablefish occur from British Columbia to Oregon, but population models show them to have undergone slight declines over the last decade. Threatened.

SALMON AND TROUT

Chinook salmon

Chinook, King, Tyee, or **Spring salmon** *(Oncorhynchus tshawytscha).* Powerful, sleek, and singularly determined to return to its birthplace to spawn and die, this salmon is at the heart of many First Nations' fishing traditions. It is also a pillar of the economy of the Pacific Northwest. Different spring runs, such as those of whitenose and blueback chinook, are said to have distinctive flavors associated with them. They are all highly valued by commercial fishermen, despite their scarcity relative to other salmon remaining along most of the Pacific coast. Chinook populations once spawned in small tributaries and headwaters throughout the region, but many of these runs have been disrupted by natural resource extraction, dams, and development. In addition, farmed and hatchery salmon may be genetically contaminating native wild runs. Some farmed and wild chinooks have been found to harbor high levels of industrial contaminants, posing a threat to indigenous and other peoples whose diets depend on the fish. Worse yet, some historically documented runs in California, Idaho, Oregon, and Washington are now extinct, while others are threatened or endangered. In Alaska, riverside access issues affect Alaskan Natives attempting to maintain their harvesting traditions.

Chum, Dog, or **Keta salmon** *(Oncorhynchus keta).* Chum salmon have the widest distribution of any Pacific salmon, with historic populations ranging from California to South Korea. They also undertake the longest migrations of any salmon species, as far as 2,100 miles up Alaska's Yukon River. Chum salmon have seen renewed interest from recreational fishermen, whose harvests of other species have been restricted in certain places. Chum have shown remarkable resilience in Washington, while other salmon species have undergone substantial declines. Most Washington runs remain viable, with the exceptions of two Puget Sound stocks that are in critical condition and lower Columbia River populations, which are declining. Further south, all Sacramento River populations are extinct. Chum remain an important staple for indigenous peoples in British Columbia and Alaska.

Coastal cutthroat trout *(Oncorhynchus clarki)*. Coastal cutthroat trout are widely distributed in Washington's lower Columbia River tributary systems and exist in many small coastal streams not suitable for other salmonids. Cutthroats are legendary among anglers, not only for the astonishing size of some prized individuals, but also for their feistiness and drive. They are appreciated by chefs for their edible skin and orange-red flesh, which retains its fine flavor and texture whether it is baked, grilled, or smoked. Above migration barriers, it is the only salmonid species present, and in small streams, it is often the only species of fish. Sadly, this esteemed sportsfish no longer has the sizeable populations along the Oregon and Washington coasts that it once did. Some populations appear vulnerable or threatened, while others appear closer to extinction.

Coho salmon

Coho or **Silver salmon** *(Oncorhynchus kisutch)*. A favorite of anglers, coho salmon typically prefer coastal streams and tributaries, which are vulnerable to the impacts of habitat degradation. Historically, populations of this species were sparsely distributed across the region, and in recent years they have comprised approximately 10 percent of the North Pacific commercial catch. Many coho runs in the south are threatened and endangered, yet management restrictions along the Oregon coast have helped to enable an upturn in abundance.

Dolly Varden char *(Salvelinus malma)*. This troutlike fish has dark blotches on its olive-brown or silver body, and can either be part of an anadromous stock, migrating between saltwater bays and freshwater streams, or a nonmigratory one, remaining in freshwater streams and lakes. It occurs from southwest Alaska through Washington, where its appearance is similar to the threatened bull trout. It is highly sought after by sports fishermen and Native American subsistence fishermen, including Alaskan Athapaskans for whom it may comprise 40 percent of their total annual fish harvest. It is smoked or eaten fresh. Its flesh is firm, pink, and full of flavor, but its spawning grounds in Alaska are now under pressure for oil exploration and development. Stocks vary in conservation status, but many are under new threats. At risk.

Pink or **Humpie (humpback) salmon** *(Oncorhynchus gorbuscha)*. Pink salmon remain the most abundant salmon species in the North Pacific. It is underpriced compared to other salmon, but its harvest is nevertheless economically critical to commercial fishermen throughout Alaska, Canada, and Washington. Pink salmon are not as important for sport fisheries as coho or chinook, but they can be caught by trolling in nearshore marine waters, along beaches, and in streams. This species features separate even-year and odd-year runs, because the individuals return to spawn after exactly two years. Parasitic sea lice infestations are negatively affecting runs in British Columbia, some of which have dramatically declined since farmed salmon appeared in their midst. All stocks in Oregon and California are now extinct.

Sockeye or **Red salmon** *(Oncorhynchus nerka)*. Sockeye are an important mainstay of many subsistence users and support several of the most important commercial fisheries on the North Pacific coast. They have been an important traditional food and ceremonial totem for the First Nations of the region, who both fire roasted them when fresh or smoked and dried them for winter use. Runs of sockeye on the Columbia and Snake Rivers

Sockeye salmon

were severely disrupted by dam building. A few runs of Puget Sound sockeye have rebounded in response to restoration efforts.

Kokanee *(Oncorhynchus nerka)*. This landlocked sockeye salmon is native to the Pacific Northwest and has been introduced to Flathead Lake, Montana and other waters beyond its natural range. As with sockeye, kokanee are sleek, silvery specimens, but with spawning, they become smooth skinned and red-colored, with large hooked jaws and teeth forming on the males. The kokanee occasionally shares spawning and rearing grounds with ocean-going sockeye and has been known to produce ocean-going offspring.

Steelhead *(Oncorhynchus mykiss)*. Steelhead are one of the most sought after sport fish in North America. The flesh has an excellent flavor and is pink in color. The life history of steelhead varies more than that of any other anadromous fish in terms of the length of time spent at sea, the length of time spent in freshwater, and the times of emigration from and immigration to freshwater. Some individuals may remain in a stream, mature, and even spawn without going to sea. Inland populations in Washington and Oregon have declined, while most coastal stocks appear to be healthy. Many California stocks are at risk.

SCULPIN

Northern Pacific sculpin (*Cottidae* spp.). At least twenty species of bottom-dwelling sculpin frequent the North Pacific, either dwelling in the tide pools of the Pacific Northwest, or in deeper, subtidal waters, often where rocky ledges and reefs occur. They were traditionally harvested by many cultures but are infrequently marketed today. As an example, see the description of cabezon, below.

Cabezon

Cabezon *(Scorpaenichthys marmoratus)*. A camouflaged bottom fish of marbled earth tones, this fish was formerly common from Baja California, to southeastern Alaska. Because males steadfastly guard nests on rocky bottoms where females lay thousands of eggs, they are unusually vulnerable to spearfishing sportsmen, and are now threatened. California has now limited commercial and recreational fishing during the spawning and nest guarding seasons.

SMELT

Eulachon or **Ooligan grease** from **candlefish** *(Thaleichthys pacificus)*. Candlefish smelt formerly moved by the millions up coastal rivers and bays to spawn on gravelly beaches, serving as a cultural keystone species whose products were linked to many culinary traditions. They form the core of an ancient but vanishing fermented-oil food tradition of the First Nations of the Pacific Northwest. Candlefish smelt were smoked and eaten, or gathered into canoes to decompose and ferment, so that their oil could be extracted and refined to mix as a preservative with berries and other foods. Some of the greatest potlatch ceremonies were ooligan "grease feasts," and different flavors of ooligan were traded into the interior for hundreds of miles as a valued medicine and food. While smelt runs in Alaska and British Columbia remained substantial through the 1940s, they have since become irregular, disrupted by coastal and riverine development as well as contamination from pollutants. By the 1990s, some runs had stopped altogether, and catches from remaining runs in British Columbia and Washington have become highly regulated. Biologists have projected that the candlefish populations can support only 28 percent of the former harvesting pressure without suffering irrevocable declines. Among the most endangered food traditions in North America.

Surf smelt *(Hypomesus pretiosus)*. This small, gray schooling fish occurs over a wide range, where it has been netted by Native Americans, dried, and eaten for centuries. It is increasingly apparent in the marketplace in the U.S. and Canada, as Asian immigrants to the Pacific Northwest have found it an analog to other smelt stocks they had known before their arrival. Although not threatened or endangered, numbers fluctuate widely from year to year, and new pressures require careful monitoring. Cultural traditions may be at risk.

SOLE AND FLOUNDER

English sole *(Pleuronectes vetulus).* Found from Mexico to Alaska, this blotchy "lemon" sole inhabits bay bottoms and estuarine environments on the Pacific coast, where it was within reach of bayside-dwelling fishing peoples. A major fishing grounds for it occurs near Hecate Straits in Canada, where it has been moderately important commercially. The English sole is caught primarily by directed trawls and marketed as filet of sole. However, its nursery and rearing grounds are in heavily contaminated bays and estuaries, and its habitat has been altered by dredging. As a result, there has been a prolonged decline in sole populations since the 1950s. English sole cover a wide range and may be healthy in some places, but in Puget Sound these bottom-feeding flatfish have suffered from the bioaccumulation of contaminants in their grayish white flesh. Some analyses suggest that when they become highly contaminated, these sole are exceedingly vulnerable to diseases and tumor growth, while their reproduction declines. Recent declines in recruitment have led biologists to suspect that thermal pollution is altering the sole's estuarine nursery grounds, particularly at the southern margin of its distribution. Catch sizes have hovered near historical lows in recent years. Increasingly rare or unsuitable for human consumption. Culturally at risk.

Heart Cockles and Family Memories

Oh, you warm the cockles of my heart!

Although a half-century on the avenues of New York City and Long Island quieted her Chester accent, my grandmother retained some of her Briticisms. Telling her grandchildren that they warmed the cockles of her heart when they ate their vegetables was one of them.

My mother used the same colorful idiom to congratulate us or encourage us to do the very thing that would push us past our comfort zone. "Oh, but you'd warm the cockles of my heart," she'd say with a loving smile...and off I just had to go. "Cockle" was a funny sounding word that meant a profound inner smile. It was a word that conjured just two images—of my grandmother and my mother. What a surprise when twenty-five years later, I learned that heart cockles were clams! They were clams that preferred quiet bays, clams that reveled in beds of eelgrass growing on mud. Clams that provided a livelihood for North America's First Nations, clams that are now threatened with extinction.

The afternoon chatter of esteemed scientists discussing threats to marine life in Salmon Nation became white noise as I swelled up with affectionate memories of my mother, and my more carefree days of being tucked in. Oh, how I would love to end today under a thick blanket, Mom's hand on my cheek, sharing the story about my day—the day I sat with a motley and passionate crew of brilliant guys and gals pulling together the first list of heritage foods in the Pacific Northwest. "Oh, they all warm the cockles of my heart," Mom (and Grandma) would've said with a lovely smile.

Makalé Faber is a food folklorist and Slow Food's Program Officer for RAFT, Presidia, and the Ark of Taste.

Petrale

Petrale *(Eopsetta jordani).* This sole lives on rocky and sandy bottoms for up to three decades. Occurring from the Bering Sea to Baja California, it was once the most sought after flatfish from Vancouver Island through areas of Puget Sound where it had been abundant. Because the average size of petrale sole has been decreasing in recent decades, direct fishing for them has been prohibited in Canada since 1995, but incidental takes are allowed. As a bottom-dwelling flatfish, the petrale sole may be vulnerable to heavy metals and other contaminants in the bays and estuaries of the Pacific Northwest. Declining in both health status and size, some populations have become unsuitable for human consumption. Culturally at risk.

Starry flounder *(Platichthys stellatus).* An oval, barred flounder that can be right-eyed or left-eyed, this species has been historically common from central California northward to the Aleutian Islands, and over to Japan and Korea. Coastal-dwelling natives and immigrants alike relish its flesh. Because it frequents flat sandy or muddy bottoms near estuaries, harbors, and marinas, it is increasingly vulnerable to pesticides in river discharges and to contamination from coastal industries and ship discharges. At risk. Some stocks unsuitable for consumption.

STURGEON

White sturgeon *(Acipenser transmontanus).* The largest freshwater fish in Canada, the century-old white sturgeon can reach eighteen feet in length and 250 pounds in weight. They formerly occurred in many rivers along the Pacific coast from California to southern Alaska but are now restricted to a few stretches of the Sacramento, Columbia, and Fraser rivers, and to a few Vancouver Island streams. In the 1880s, one million pounds of white sturgeon were harvested from the lower Columbia in a matter of a few years, and another two hundred thousand pounds from the Fraser in the 1890s. The Fraser fishery was entirely closed in 1994, after declining annual harvests of only two thousand to eight thousand pounds. White sturgeon have limited access to historic spawning grounds and to the animal foods they require for their diets. They are now so endangered that First Nations peoples have voluntarily abstained from subsistence harvests until the species recovers.

Green sturgeon *(Acipenser medirostris).* Green sturgeon are long-lived, achieve sizes of up to seven feet in length, and have had a long tenure on this planet. Their dark-colored meat was once valued for its mild flavor and a texture likened to that of veal, but in recent decades it has fallen into obscurity among younger chefs who have never been exposed to it. Population analyses reviewed by the American Fisheries Society suggest that this species has declined by 88 percent over its range during the era of replicable censuses, and may be headed toward extinction unless drastic interventions are undertaken. Occasionally, it is still brought in along with white sturgeon off the coasts of Oregon and Washington.

MARINE ALGAE

Nori, Purple, or **Red laver** (*Porphyra abbottiae* and other *Porphyra* spp.). A thin, membranous, reddish purple alga, red laver has a texture and translucence like cellophane when it is fresh. However, when it is dried for later use, its former translucence becomes obscured by dark green and blackish hues, and its texture becomes brittle. Widespread on rocks in the intertidal zone from Alaska southward to California, it was gathered by coastal tribes at low tide in the spring. It is extremely nutritious, containing virtually the full range of essential nutrients. The plants are harvested from the rocks, sun-dried, and sometimes further processed by pressing moistened cakes into cedar boxes for several days before chopping and redrying. Elaborate preparation methods developed among several coastal tribes (for example, Kwakwaka'wakw, Heiltsuk, Coast Tsimshian, Haida, and Tlingit), who served red laver with chum salmon, ooligan grease, halibut, or boiled clams. Historically, a common gift from coastal tribes to inland tribes or to the Chinese was a bag of this seaweed, for it was valued as a treatment for goiter (iodine deficiency). Still used on the central and north coasts, it is declining as a food tradition in the south, except among Asian immigrants. There are concerns of contamination and of commercial harvests that will deplete it and reduce access. At risk as a food tradition.

Giant kelp (*Macrocystis integrifolia*). Among the largest marine algae, this brown kelp clings to rocks in the upper subtidal zone, where Pacific herring deposit thick layers of spawn on its blades from March to June. Although this brown alga occurs throughout the world, a unique tradition developed in Salmon Nation of harvesting the spawn-covered blades. The dried blades were formerly stored or traded, then soaked and boiled in cedar boxes and eaten

Giant kelp

with ooligan grease. Endangered as a tradition due to declining harvests.

SHELLFISH (MOLLUSCS)

ABALONE

Flat abalone *(Haliotis walallensis)*. In a flattened, narrow, low-ribbed shell, this abalone is mottled yellow and brown, and sometimes reaches seven inches in breadth. Ranging from British Columbia southward to southern California, this species is found in subtidal zones from twenty to fifty feet in depth. The minimum commercial size limit for this species in California has been set at four inches. Although its harvest has not been closed as it has been for blacks, pinks, greens, and whites, this abalone is threatened and in possible decline throughout much of its range.

Pinto or **Northern Pacific abalone** *(Haliotis kamtschatkana)*. This northernmost abalone has a thin, mottled shell with a reddish or greenish cast, and once reached ten inches in breadth, although any over seven inches are now a rare find. It occurs from Alaska to Baja California, and lives deeper than other Pacific abalones. Although once used sustainably for sustenance, it is now considered threatened in Canada and the U.S., in part due to commercial overexploitation by scuba divers between 1960 and 1991, when harvests were closed in Canada. A restrictive season—sometimes only six days long—is still allowed in Alaska, where harvests have declined from 315,000 pounds in 1978–79 to 37,000 pounds in 1993–94. Declines may be due to commercial overharvesting combined with sports fishing by scuba divers, expanding sea otter populations, and declining kelp populations. Illegal poaching continues to affect its populations. Endangered.

Red abalone *(Haliotis rufescens)*. The epipodium—or underside edge—of this primarily Californian species can be solid black, or barred with black and cream. It occurs from Sunset Bay, Oregon, southward to Baja California, reaching a foot in diameter on rare occasions, and therefore receiving honors as the world's largest abalone. It has been used by indigenous peoples for eight thousand years or more, and is now farmed for most culinary uses. Commercial harvesting is prohibited south of San Francisco Bay in California and only allowed in Oregon by permit for use as broodstock.

CRUSTACEAN

Dungeness crab *(Cancer magister)*. This signature Northwestern food may vary in abundance, but it serves as an example of a vibrant food tradition still widely recognized in and beyond the region. Named for a fishing village along the Strait of Juan de Fuca, it has been commercially harvested and featured in Salmon Nation as a heritage food since the late 1800s. Its distribution

Dungeness crab

runs from California to Alaska. While there is growing competition among cultures for this prized food, it is still common in places where viable traditions appear intact.

Pacific northern shrimp *(Pandalus jordani)*. One of the most important commercial species of shrimp in the world, this coldwater species is sweet tasting and some consider it to be more flavorful and moist than the common Atlantic *borealis*. A variety of gear types are used to harvest these shrimp along the West Coast, including traps, otter trawls, and one-beam trawls. Most of the harvest occurs close to shore. Pacific northern shrimp sold in the U.S. market are primarily from the stretch of coast between northern California and southeast Alaska. This species is vulnerable and threatened by heavy fishing and wasting as bycatch.

OTHER BIVALVE (CLAM, COCKLE, AND MUSSEL)

Geoduck *(Panopea abrupta)*. The major traditional harvest of the largest burrowing clam in the world takes place around Puget Sound, but the hard shells of this species have turned up as far south as Baja California, and as far north as Alaska. The common name is a minor corruption of a Native American term and is often pronounced "gooey-duck." For indigenous peoples of the Pacific Northwest, the tidal flats yielded prodigious quantities of

Geoduck

geoduck, each large enough to make a meal for six. Today, the majority of geoduck harvested commercially is shipped live to Asian markets, where it is prized for its sweet flavor and crunchy texture. Until Canada set individual quotas for geoduck beds, collectors were exceeding sustainability targets by more than 80 percent. Tribes in the U.S. and Canada are managing tidal lands for geoduck, while at least five Canadian operations are now farming them. Common in parts of Puget Sound, they are at risk in accessible areas due to intensive digging pressure and persist only at the extreme low tide line. Honored on Slow Food's Ark of Taste.

Pacific goose or **Leaf barnacle** *(Pollicipes polymerus)*. Found clustered together like thatching on wave-exposed rocks in the middle intertidal zone from British Columbia to Baja California, these peculiar shellfish are distinguished by their long "goose necks," or edible stalks, that stick out from their plated shells. They grow up to six inches in length and have a delicious meat inside them. Folk tales suggest that geese emerge from these shellfish and their European counterparts. Unfortunately, they are quite vulnerable to contamination and have been severely impacted by oil spills near San Francisco and Santa Barbara. Nevertheless their populations have remained stable or have recovered enough in some areas to allow for open, year-round seasons, with allowable harvests set at ten pounds whole or five pounds of edible barnacle stalks. Not threatened but vulnerable to pollution and in recovery from it.

Pacific razor clam

Pacific razor clam *(Siliqua patula).* This clam can be found from California to Alaska and has been harvested both near beaches exposed to violent wave action and those along more protected shorelines. The volume of clam meat offered by this species is substantial, and it is an old favorite among specialty seafood restaurants in Salmon Nation. Its soft shells are easily smashed by indiscriminate diggers who, in some places free of recent red tides, continue to cause illegal damage to populations. A biotoxin from a microbe called Psuedonitzschia was discovered in the early 1980s. It caused mass mortalities of large numbers of clams and can cause paralytic shellfish poisoning (PSP) in humans. It is unknown how long this disease has affected clam populations. Traditional harvesting practices are in decline and at risk.

Scallop *(Argopecten, Chlamys, Crassadoma,* and *Patinopecten* spp.). Although too small to support commercial fisheries, these diverse scallops are harvested by sports divers. However, bay closures have been triggered by sewage contamination and toxins, including PSP. Threatened by pollution limiting its culinary use.

Butter clam

Butter clam *(Saxidomus giganteus).* Butter clams are native to the protected bays and estuaries of the Pacific Northwest and are an important commercial and sport clam. Many people consider them the best for chowder. Most of the butter clams harvested from the intertidal zone of Salmon Nation are taken by hand, and taking undersized ones is strictly prohibited in many places. This traditional hand harvesting appears not to disturb many other intertidal invertebrates. The remaining populations are diminishing and at risk, due to the long-term effects of oil spills, biotoxins, and other contamination. Now providing less than 10 percent of the commercial intertidal clam harvest in Salmon Nation, sewage pollution and PSP have closed large areas of the coast to harvesting.

Littleneck clam *(Protothaca staminea).* First Nations tribesmen of the Pacific Northwest still recall how Raven first discovered humans hidden in the shell of a littleneck clam. Often found intermingled with butter clams, these "steamers" now make up less then one-tenth of the total clam harvest along the Pacific coast.

Delicious when steamed open and dipped in hot butter, they are an important part of the heritage of many coastal communities and a key factor in rural economies — historic harvests were in the tens of millions of pounds per year in the Pacific Northwest. Now, however, pollution from oil spills has caused declines in and the closure of certain clamming beds, with hundreds of thousands of dollars of revenue now being lost annually by the Lummi Indians alone. Littlenecks persist in the fresh markets of the Pacific Northwest but access to uncontaminated clam beds has declined dramatically. Threatened as a tradition.

Heart cockle *(Clinocardium nuttallii).* This clam prefers those portions of quiet bays in which the substratum consists of muddy, fine sand, though beds of eelgrass growing on mud also support large populations. Cockles are taken by clam diggers, especially those of First Nations but are now seldom harvested commercially. They range from Alaska to Mexico. Now they are found at lower densities, with smaller average sizes per cockle, than were recorded a decade ago in the same cockle beds. Sewage pollution and PSP have closed large areas of coast to harvesting. Declining and threatened.

Heart cockle

Horse, Gaper, or **Great Washington clam** *(Schizothaerus nuttallii).* Often confused with the geoduck, horse clams are large rubbernecks that develop in thin, chalky white shells. Their large siphon, which is capable of great extension, provides most of the meat, and is skinned and pounded or ground, usually for chowder. Indians formerly dried the siphons for winter use. Similar to the slightly smaller gray-neck *(Schizothaerus capax),* the two species are not usually separated in catch statistics. They appear fairly often in sport catches but are of minor commercial importance. These clams were prehistorically cultivated by coastal communities of First Nations peoples but are now suffering in both Washington and British Columbia from contamination and downward population trends. Threatened, and at continued risk.

Horse clam

Soft-shell clam or **Soft-shell mussel** *(Mya arenaria).* These clams were commonly found in freshwater river mouths and brackish bays in Washington, Oregon, British Columbia, and Alaska after their introduction in the 1870s. They became an important food for most river peoples of the region but are now contaminated by a variety of toxins, including PSP. Threatened.

CEPHALOPOD

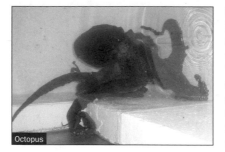
Octopus

Octopus or **Devil fish** *(Octopus dofleini)*. Historically, this species was eaten raw as well as used for halibut bait on hand-carved hooks that sometimes held images of its tentacles. This common octopus of the Pacific coast can be depleted by trawling and by inter- and subtidal rock disruption by divers and tide pool scavengers. Eaten historically by a number of native and immigrant cultures, this species is now at risk of overexploitation.

OYSTER

Olympia oyster *(Ostrea lurida)*. Formerly abundant, the Olympia oyster was an important food source for many coastal Native American tribes. In response to the overharvesting of native oysters that occurred around Puget Sound and adjacent coastal areas up through the Civil War, a few oystermen decided to augment their harvests by introducing the faster growing Japanese oyster to the area. These larger, more voracious, exotic oysters were soon outcompeting the native Olympia, which were further diminished by non-native predators and pollution. In recent decades there has been some recovery of native populations where water quality has improved, but they are believed to be below precontact levels. Efforts are underway both to reintroduce them to sites where they formerly occurred and to enhance surviving populations. Honored on Slow Food USA's Ark of Taste.

Introduced "Japanese" oyster *(Crassostrea gigas)*. Intentionally brought to the Pacific Northwest coast by several immigrant groups since 1905, these are the large cupped oysters that originated in Asia, Japan, and New Zealand. They have adapted to local coastal conditions, and each localities' oysters have a distinctive taste. Consider the status of some of the better-known non-native oysters, below:

Introduced "Japanese" oyster

Hamma Hamma oyster *(Crassostrea gigas)*. This variety of oyster is farmed at the site of one of the biggest historic aquaculture concentrations in the U.S., and is offered by the wholesaler, Hamma Hamma Company Store, which also grows its own clams.

Quilcenes oyster *(Crassostrea gigas)*. Derived from what has been the world's largest oyster hatchery, this high quality oyster was developed in Quilcene, Washington, in 1978.

Snow Creek oyster *(Crassostrea gigas)*. These diminutive oysters grow inside delicate, striped shells and are now being farmed in Salmon Nation. Their tender meat has a creamy texture and a sweet flavor. Some aficionados claim that Snow Creek oysters have a taste that seems "pure" compared to other oysters, while others marvel how they "pulse" on the tongue. They are farmed around Snow Creek, from Port Angeles to Discovery Bay, Washington.

Umpqua Flats oyster *(Crassostrea gigas)*. Now being farmed in Salmon Nation, this is a rather tender oyster with a paradoxical flavor that is simultaneously sweet and briny. It may be medium to long in overall size but has a tiny heart that gives it a special beauty.

Yaquina oyster *(Crassostrea gigas)*. These oysters range in size but are always meaty. This unique stock was first recorded in Salmon Nation during the shipwreck of the *Schooner Juliet* in 1852; by 1863, two oyster harvesting companies had opened businesses around "Oysterville" on Yaquina Bay. By 1907, Oregon Oyster Farms used the stock in the area to produce oysters for restaurants in Portland.

WILD FOODS

FERNS

Spiny woodfern *(Dryopteris expansa)*. A perennial with triangular fronds almost two feet in height, this spiny fern has large rhizomes that were formerly harvested in fall and winter, when the plants were dormant. Pit-roasted, steamed, or boiled in kettles, the bitter rhizomes become sweet tasting, like yams. The spiny woodfern grows from sea level to tree line along the Pacific coast west of the Cascades. It was once very important among many peoples, including the Haida, Nuxalk (Bella Coola), Nlaka'pmx (Thompson), and Gitxkan not only as a food but as a cure for those who ate poisonous plants or shellfish infected with the red tide. This historic food is apparently no longer used at all among the dozen cultures that once relished it. It is culturally endangered as a tradition, although the plant itself remains widespread.

Fiddlehead or **Ostrich fern** *(Matteuccia struthiopteris)*. The most commercially marketed fern, it grows from north-central British Columbia into Oregon. It is still harvested extensively but apparently not traditionally by First Nations. Several restaurants in Salmon Nation have featured fiddleheads from this fern as a signature food. Not at risk.

Fiddlehead fern

Licorice fern *(Polypodium glycyrrhiza)*. The rhizomes of this fern contain a compound—Polypodoside A—that is six hundred times sweeter than sugar by weight. It has long been used by First Peoples of northwestern North America as an appetizer, mouth sweetener, and for sweetening beverages and medicinal teas. Some people still use it, but its traditions have declined and are at risk.

Licorice fern

FUNGI

Fir bolete *(Boletus abieticola).* In most states and provinces of Salmon Nation, this wood decomposer is not commercially harvested to any extent but is widely used as food. Not at risk.

Queen bolete or **Moretti** *(Boletus aureus).* Used as food, as a decorative, or as forage, this bolete is harvested commercially in Oregon and northern California. It is rich in vitamins B, C, and niacin. Not at risk.

Butter bolete *(Boletus appendiculatus).* Known from California, Idaho, and Oregon, this bolete is not often harvested commercially, but it is a delectable edible for hobbyists. Not at risk.

Admirable bolete *(Boletus mirabilis).* Found in most states and provinces within Salmon Nation, this gold-capped bolete is harvested commercially as food, forage, and as a decorative. Not at risk.

Red-capped butter bolete *(Boletus regius).* Found only in northern California, Oregon, Washington, and adjacent Canada, this red-capped mushroom is not currently harvested commercially but valued as food by recreational collectors. Not at risk.

Rainbow chanterelle *(Cantharellus cibarius var. roseocanus).* This multicolored variety of the golden chanterelle is plentiful, and commercially harvested for food from Alaska, through British Columbia and into Washington and Oregon. A firm, meaty mushroom with an apricot aroma, it can grow to six inches in height, and weigh up to one half-pound. Not at risk.

White chanterelle

White chanterelle *(Cantharellus subalbidus).* Ranging from Alaska through western Canada southward to California, this white-tinged mushroom is commercially harvested in several states and provinces. Not at risk.

Bear's head

Bear's head *(Hericium abietis).* Found from Alaska through western Canada and the interior of the Columbia River watershed, this mushroom is commercially harvested. Not at risk.

Slimy-top mushroom *(Hygrophorus gliocyclus)*. Traditionally harvested and eaten by Interior Salish peoples of the Fraser and Columbian plateaus, this slippery mushroom is little-known or used today. Because it is rarely seen even among mycologists, its traditions are at risk.

Lobster mushroom *(Hypomyces lactifluorum)*. Curiously, this

Lobster mushroom

parasite grows on *Russula brevipes* in the Cascades and other uplands in six states and provinces. It is commercially harvested, and not at risk.

Oregon black truffle *(Picoa carthusiana)*. A world-class truffle with a haunting but delicious flavor that heightens from mild to pungent with after-ripening. Though not necessarily encountered by all mushroom foragers, it is not at risk.

Salmon Nation Foods as Medicines

"Our Food is Our Medicine!" I have heard this statement so many times in my work with indigenous elders and cultural specialists around Salmon Nation. For these people, food is so much more than calories or vitamins; food is a part of their very identity, part of their existence.

Without their traditional foods, whether these are wild berries, root vegetables, seaweed, or eulachen (ooligan) grease, some portion of their very being is lost. Furthermore, they emphasize, harvesting and preparing these different foods keeps a whole system of knowledge alive that has been passed from generation to generation for thousands of years — vital information and experience about seasons, places, relationships to other animals and plants, and caring for their home places.

It is no wonder that these people feel bitterness toward those individuals, governments, and institutions who have alienated them from their lands and food sources and have prevented them from caring for their environments. They look with alarm at the pollution, overharvesting, and environmental destruction wrought by industrial development, and they strive to preserve what they can of the food species and the lifeways that allow these species to flourish and yet still be used, with care and respect. They regard the continuation of these food traditions as their responsibility to their families, communities, and habitats. This is why it is important for all of us to help preserve, restore, and maintain the rich array of foods of Salmon Nation.

Nancy J. Turner is a Canadian ethnobotanist honored with the Slow Food Award for Biodiversity in 2000.

Cottonwood mushroom *(Tricholoma populinum)*. Traditionally harvested by Interior Salish peoples of the Fraser and Columbian plateaus, this is an exceptionally good tasting species that grows in autumn under cottonwood trees *(Populus balsamifera* ssp. *trichocarpa)*; formerly dried, it is now jarred or frozen for winter. While not used commercially, it is not at risk.

Cottonwood mushroom

Pine mushroom

Pine mushroom *(Tricholoma magnivelare)*. Traditionally harvested by Interior Salish peoples of the Fraser and Columbian plateaus, and exceptionally good tasting, the pine mushroom grows in summer and fall under coniferous trees. Formerly sliced and dried for storage, it is now jarred or frozen. Harvested commercially, especially in the Skeena and Nass valleys, it is not at risk.

Oregon white truffle *(Tuber gibbosum)*. Found in the wild and farmed under inoculated Douglas fir seedlings, this small truffle is tan, not white. Its aroma and flavors become more complex with age. It is not at risk.

GRAINS OR GRASSLIKE PLANTS

Eelgrass

Eelgrass *(Zostera marina)*. This true seagrass has edible leaf bases and rhizomes used in different parts of its range along northern Pacific coasts. Eelgrass formerly formed extensive seagrass beds in shoals and bays near open ocean water and estuaries. It is still widely distributed along the Pacific coast in areas where the coastline or estuaries have not been highly modified; in some cases, it is locally abundant. The coastal Salish used the rhizomes in steaming pits to flavor deer, seal, or dolphin meat. The Kwakwaka'wakw favored the rhizomes, stems, and leaf-bases raw, gathering them with long twisting poles from canoes at low tides in May. The availability of this marine food plant has been impacted by dredging, trawling, and contamination from industrial aquaculture, among other threats. Its use is infrequent now, and because of contamination, cultural traditions surrounding its use are at risk.

"INDIAN POTATOES" AND OTHER WILD ROOT OR STEM VEGETABLES

Balsamroot or **Spring sunflower** *(Balsamorhiza sagittata)*. This plant grows widely in grasslands and open woodlands of the interior of southern British Columbia south to Oregon and California. Like Jerusalem artichokes, the balsamroot has inulin as its major carbohydrate; when the roots are pit-cooked, the inulin converts to fructose and fructans, making the cooked roots sweet tasting and more digestible than when raw. Only the young, carrot-sized roots are edible; the larger ones are too woody. The leafy shoots are edible before they emerge in spring,

and the young flower bud stalks and leaf stalks can also be peeled and eaten fresh or cooked. Its small achenes, tasting like greenish sunflower seeds, can be eaten raw and were formerly ground into meal and cooked in soups and stews. This multiple-use edible plant is scarcely used at all today. Although the plants are still common, their traditions are at risk.

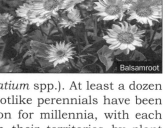

Balsamroot

Biscuitroot, Desert parsley, and other names (*Lomatium* spp.). At least a dozen species of these short, yellow- or white-flowered, carrotlike perennials have been used as food in various watersheds of Salmon Nation for millennia, with each tribe discerning the different species or varieties in their territories by plant morphology and shape. Biscuitroot plants were marked in the summer during flowering, and their tapering or tuberous taproots dug up the following spring, with smaller ones returned to the soil for regeneration. The young shoots and leaves of some species were also eaten. The roots are sweet to somewhat sharp-tasting, and eaten raw or cooked, with different species found in special ecological niches throughout the region. Traditions are currently recovering in a few places due to cultural revitalization of "root feasts." Although the most commonly utilized species (for example *Lomatium canbyi, L. cous, L. dissectum, L. macrocarpum, L. nudicaule)* are widespread and abundant in patches, several other species are now on state "watch lists" and are at risk.

Biscuitroot

Bitterroot *(Lewisia rediviva).* This tap-rooted, pink-flowered perennial grows in dry sagebrush areas and open pine woods; it is the state flower of Montana. The roots were once dug in large quantities by Interior Plateau peoples from the Okanagan valley southwards. Harvested in spring before the plants flowered, the roots were peeled and dried for winter use and trade. They are still highly valued, but populations have been dramatically diminished from grazing, agriculture, and urban development. Endangered as a food tradition.

Bitterroot

Blue camas *(Camassia quamash).* This beautiful blue-flowered lily produces glutinous edible bulbs about the size of sweet chestnuts. It is an herbaceous perennial, growing in wet meadows, prairies, and grassy bluffs from British Columbia, Washington, Oregon, and northern California back into Alberta, Idaho,

Blue camas

and Montana. This important staple was semicultivated in traditional gathering grounds of dozens of Salmon Nation peoples, some of whom maintain camas festivals and are involved in restoration and salvage projects for camas. The Pit River tribe now burns meadows to enhance camas populations. Steamed in pits for days, camas bulbs become sweet, soft, and brownish in color, and have been used to sweeten other foods. Straits Salish formerly traded it to Fraser River tribes. There are special populations of blue camas that grow in a few estuarine tidal marshes (such as Alberni Inlet) that were particularly relished. Recovering through cultural revitalization in some areas but still very much at risk as a tradition.

Giant camas *(Camassia leichtlinii).* This more robust plant has larger bulbs than the blue camas but is not as common. Restricted to Oregon, Vancouver Island, and the Gulf Islands, it begins blooming about two weeks later than common camas, and grows considerably taller. By pit-roasting its inulin-rich bulbs, their complex carbohydrates are converted to sweet fructose and fructans. The traditions associated with giant camas are no longer commonly practiced within its narrow range, and are culturally at risk. Furthermore, the plant is considered rare in the British Columbia part of its range. Like *C. quamash,* it was formerly managed through the clearing and burning of areas to maintain prairie habitats. Giant camas are an important wildlife food.

Chocolate lily *(Fritillaria lanceolata).* Related to riceroot, this herbaceous perennial produces edible white bell-shaped bulbs with surrounding ricelike bulblets. It grows in meadows and on grassy bluffs, often in association with blue camas, over a wide stretch of Salmon Nation, from Washington to Alaska. Steamed in pits or metal pots, chocolate lily bulbs have a tender, delicate (though sometimes bitter) taste. It is clearly at risk, as its cultural use has declined.

Chocolate lily

Cow parsnip *(Heracleum lanatum).* This hairy, large-stalked plant in the celery family is sometimes called "Indian rhubarb" or Indian celery. The young stalks of the flower buds and leaves provide a springtime vegetable with a juicy, celerylike flavor and texture but must always be peeled before being eaten. It occurs in moist open meadows, roadsides, and floodplains from sea level to tree line along the Pacific coast and in the interior. Its skin must be

Cow parsnip

peeled because it contains concentrations of phototoxins that can cause severe skin irritation and discoloring. Once peeled, the stalks are eaten raw or cooked. Widespread, and still abundant, cow parsnip remains a popular spring tonic of nutritional importance to several tribes in Salmon Nation. Recovering in a few places but still at risk as a tradition.

Hooker's onion

Hooker's onion *(Allium acuminatum).* With very thin, grasslike leaves and small spherical bulbs under a netlike skin, this wild onion grows in rocky crevices and sandy soil on dry slopes in coastal forests. This wild onion is restricted to the dry slopes of coastal forests, especially on the Gulf Islands. Coastal Salish tribes marked the plants in the spring for late summer and fall harvest. They are eaten raw or steamed in pits lined with pine or alder boughs. Called the "elder brothers" of fiddlenecks, their traditions among many tribes are in decline and are at risk.

Nodding onion *(Allium cernuum).* This beautiful pink-flowered onion with pink-tinged, elongated bulbs and thin, fleshy leaves is a favorite of the First Nations of the Interior Plateau. They formerly harvested the bulbs in quantity in the spring, before flowering, and pit-cooked them, rendering them sweet tasting and delicious. Few people still gather them today but interest in their use is increasing. Nodding onion are still common, but they are reduced in size and abundance relative to their historic status. Their productivity has recently been enhanced by burning, so some recovery is taking place.

Mountain potato

Mountain potato or **Spring beauty** *(Claytonia lanceolata).* The spherical underground corms of this gorgeous wildflower are delicious and were formerly served as a staple vegetable throughout much of the plant's range. These "potatoes" were harvested in large quantities from montane meadows and subalpine forests and hillsides throughout Salmon Nation, where they often grew with the yellow glacier lily *(Erythronium grandiflorum).* Stored fresh, or strung and dried, they were steamed before eating. Once very important for Tsilhqut'in tribal members living around the Potato Mountain range in central British Columbia, they are little used today. Elders now claim that since the time of their youth, the average corm size has declined. They attribute this to impacts of cattle grazing and lack of tending by people. There is great interest in increasing its use, but its traditions remain at risk.

Northern riceroot

Northern riceroot, Indian rice, or **Missionbells** *(Fritillaria camschatcensis).* This dark-purple to (rarely) yellowish flowered herbaceous perennial of tidal marshes, upland meadows, and moist coastal bluffs has large bulbs comprised of masses of ricelike bulblets—sometimes over one hundred per bulb. It ranges from Washington north to Alaska, where it can be found in abundance along the coast. The bulbs have been steamed or boiled by most coastal tribes. They were particularly valued by the Kwakwaka'wakw, Haisla, Tsimshian, Haida, and Tlingit on the Northwest coast, and were steamed and eaten with oil and sometimes with "wild rhubarb" (western dock) leaves. In some areas the plants were cultivated and their growth promoted by replanting the bulblets and basal shoots growing from the main bulbs. They are also known as a food of geese and ducks. However, among the dozen or so tribes that formerly used them, few have used them at anytime over the last half-century. Although the food plant remains common within certain habitats, many areas where they formerly grew have been damaged by industrial development in river estuaries. This food is endangered as a cultural tradition, although there is interest in many communities in reviving its use.

Pacific silverweed or **Cinquefoil** *(Potentilla anserina* ssp. *pacifica).* This wild vegetable has leaves that are often silvery white on their undersides, with spreading runners, and two kinds of edible roots. Shorter, curly roots are just below the

Speaking to Our Roots

Memories of the dinner tables of the older longhouses of my childhood did not foretell our loss, especially of our nourishment, blood strength, and birthright. Our litany at meals expresses gratitude to purity of Water, Deer, Salmon, Roots, and Berries. The elder people of my childhood spoke of continuance as responsibility to all life. We still call their names out loud in grace.

In the Warm Springs nation's statement of sovereignty, my people wrote: "For millennia, Warm Springs people followed an elaborate structure of sovereign tribal responsibilities embodied in the Ichiskiin phrase, *tee-cha-meengsh-mee sin-wit na-me- ah-wa-ta-man-wit*... at the time of creation the Creator placed us in this land. He gave us the voice of this land and that is our law." The tribes of the Columbia River "possessed the sovereign prerogative of *ne-shy-chut*.... Native Warm Springs people were rooted in the soil of their ancestral domain free of any outside forces, free to follow their own culture and religion."

Our ancestors possessed an agreement with the food chiefs to protect and care for their kind and heartlands. Family and clans bore senior responsibility for interabundance. Codes of conduct stood the test of time. My ancestors reserved in treaty these rights to fish, hunt, and gather at "usual and accustomed places." Even though one side of this treaty was an "infant and unreliable" government, our ancestors believed in the value of keeping agreements. Our universal human frailty is denial of the obvious and not caring.

If one story can illustrate the profane

ground surface, but longer, thicker taproots grow down to some depth below the foliage. Harvested from tidal marshes and mudflats, usually when the leaves die back in the fall, this species grows in extensive patches that were often formerly "owned and cultivated" by tribal chiefs. Somewhat bitter when raw, the roots are steamed in cedar boxes or pit-roasted at ritual feasts of several coastal tribes, and are also used for everyday meals. Traditional harvesting and feasting with these roots has been in decline. While there are several efforts underway to recover their use, traditions remain at risk.

Pink fawn lily *(Erythronium revolutum).* This pale, pink-flowered nodding lily has elongated bulbs below the soil surface of sandy meadows and forest openings. Although it ranges from British Columbia through northern California, it is considered rare in many places. The milky, slightly bitter taste of the raw bulbs was improved by drying then boiling them, or steaming them in cedar boxes. It has apparently fallen out of use, and is barely remembered among the Kwakwaka'wakw (Kwakiutl) and the Nuu-Chah-Nulth of Vancouver Island. Threatened, with traditional use in steep decline.

Pink slipper orchid

Pink slipper or **False lady's slipper orchid** *(Calypso bulbosa).* Below solitary, rose-colored flowers and a single leaf lies a white globular corm hidden below the duff on the forest floor. This wide-ranging orchid survives from sea level to 4,200 feet. The Haida ate this root vegetable raw,

oppression of people, especially native people and their independence, it is about food and food security. The loss of millions of salmon, buffalo, and rich soils, the near extirpation of whales, and the desertification of native plants and medicines are facts. Indigenous peoples went mum to protect these foods and now must capture the world's attention on how integral these species are to the balance of reciprocity. Starvation is still a threat as foods indigenous to Salmon Nation's lands and waters perish, and as rapid dietary changes in two generations imperil the native peoples with heart disease, diabetes, and cancer. Corporatized and controlled, [the other kind of] American food is imperiling life.

In my childhood, like that of many other friends in Salmon Nation, these foods seemed plentiful. In reality, we were seeing and tasting the last vestiges of some plants and animals. It was the beginning of scarcity of indigenous food. My Nisqually elder Billy Frank, Jr. went to jail over fifty times for fishing. No one counted the times he was beaten by police and game wardens. The real struggle we now face is how to see the continuance of Salmon Nation's food communities, their watersheds and homelands. We must frame this struggle in basic human rights for it to matter to most. Each ecosystem has a hero like Billy Frank, Jr. Sometimes it is only a child gathering roots for her grandmother in a nearby field. That little girl will speak to her roots, and gently bring them into the light—into her diet—without disruption of their neighbors. All of us can delight in her grandmother's thanks that at least some of these traditions continue.

Elizabeth Woody is a Native American poet and Director of the Indigenous Leadership Program at Ecotrust.

nicknaming it "black cod grease." It may no longer be in frequent use. This is a declining tradition, which remains at risk.

Poque or **Groundcone** *(Boschniakia hookeri).* This purple parasitic broomrape grows mainly on salal. Its round, cormlike base was historically eaten by several coastal tribes in British Columbia and had the flavor of some potatoes. It has fallen into disuse and is endangered as a food tradition.

Springbank clover

Springbank clover *(Trifolium wormskjoldii).* This wild perennial clover is a food of tidal marshes, low dunes, and estuaries, where it produces long, trailing white rhizomes. It occurs from Alaska to Puget Sound along the coast. Formerly semicultivated as an important vegetable for Coast Salish, Kwakwaka'wakw, Haisla, and the Haida, families traditionally managed patches of springbank clover near river mouths, in some cases distinguishing two varieties. They boiled, steamed, or pit-cooked the rhizomes as a staple root vegetable along with Pacific silverweed roots and camas bulbs, and ate them together with salmon roe, or dried salmon in highly ritualized as well as everyday meals. At risk culturally, with some populations at biological risk from habitat destruction and competition from invasive species, including European white clover.

Wapato

Wapato or **Duck potato** *(Sagittaria latifolia).* An emergent herbaceous plant of wetlands, with large, arrow-shaped leaves, wapato was a historically important staple that was stored and traded. Its starchy tubers were dug up, peeled, sliced, and eaten as "swamp potatoes." Although the duck potato is found throughout North America, its food traditions are strongest in the Northwest, where Lewis and Clark first reported them in 1806. Indigenous families and clans formerly managed particular wapato stands along slow-moving streams and in quiet, shallow lakes. Wapato is now being propagated as several tribes participate in wildlands restoration and wetlands construction. One of the most important starchy staples of Salmon Nation, its cream-colored flesh is slightly bitter when raw. When cooked, wapato offers a pleasant, nutty flavor so similar to Idaho potatoes that one potato chip company has considered marketing it. Recovering due to cultural revitalization, it is still at risk as a tradition, especially near certain contaminated wetlands, where it may be concentrating toxins in its tubers.

Water parsnip *(Sium suave)*. A perennial herb of swamps and shallow waters off lake edges, this plant produces clusters of long, fleshy roots that resemble miniature parsnips, which were historically harvested along with wapato. Both the stems and roots have been eaten raw or cooked by many tribes of Salmon Nation, but other plant parts may be poisonous [Note that it has a similar appearance to the drastically poisonous water hemlock—*Cicuta* species, and sometimes grows together with this plant]. Although not biologically threatened, its populations have been restricted through habitat destruction and pollution, and cultural traditions have atrophied. Endangered as a cultural tradition, it faces continuing risks.

Yampa *(Perideridia gairdneri)*. This white-flowered, carbohydrate-rich, wild root crop grows from California through Canada, favoring wet meadows and open prairie soils below rocky outcrops. There is evidence that decades of forest fire suppression have allowed woodlands to encroach upon yampa meadows, reducing its abundance in open habitats. It is little-known or used today in much of its range. Endangered as a cultural tradition, facing continuing risks.

Yampa

Yellow glacier lily *(Erythronium grandiflorum)*. The elongated bulbs of this lily resemble bear's teeth. They were harvested in quantity from the upland slopes and open woodlands of the Interior Plateau region, especially by the northern Interior Salish, Tsilhqut'in, and Ktunaxa. The bulbs were steamed, or more commonly pit-cooked, then dried for winter use and trade. They have a sweet taste and were a major source of carbohydrates. They were formerly maintained by burning. Their use has declined significantly, and their productivity has been impacted by overgrazing and development as well as from fire suppression. Endangered as a cultural tradition.

Yellow glacier lily

Yellowbells *(Fritillaria pudica)*. This relative of riceroot with edible bulbs has solitary yellow flowers, and occurs from grasslands through pine forests from Nevada and California northward to Alberta and British Columbia. The small, white bulb is rich in starch, and Interior tribes used it raw like a potato, or cooked as a ricelike starch. They sometimes dried it for later use. Although it can be harvested in May, it was often used in the fall when it was boiled with bitterroot. Yellowbells can be eaten raw or cooked, with very different culinary results. When served raw, yellowbell bulbs are often likened to potatoes, jicama, and other root crops; when baked, they lose their crispness, and the resulting texture and flavor are more akin to rice. The tender, immature seed capsules or pods of this species can be boiled and eaten as a wild green. However, they are bitter to the taste even after cooking, and acceptable largely to those people who favor bitter herbs. Although still available in the wild, the Sahaptin speaking people and other Interior peoples no longer use it. Endangered as a cultural tradition.

Sea bean, Salty horn, or **Criste marine** *(Salicornia maritima).* This succulent-leaved halophyte can grow in brackish estuaries or in the fresh water of river mouths, and is extremely abundant within Salmon Nation. It has been eaten in the region for thousands of years and was found in the digestive tract of the Canadian Ice Man. Now being marketed commercially, its use is recovering.

MARINE MAMMALS

PINNIPED

Spotted seal

Harbor or **Spotted seal** *(Phoca vitulina).* A boreal and low-Arctic species that is nonmigratory in most of its range, this seal of open seas ranges southward into Alaska and Canada, where it avoids masses of solid ice. The seals appear close to land only in late summer and fall, when they bask and play around brackish lagoons and bays, lingering on sandbars at river mouths. There, indigenous hunters traditionally pursued them with skin-covered umiak kayaks, or from blinds constructed on the sandbars and rocky shores; an ancient tradition of netting harbor seals has all but died out. Estimates for harbor seal population sizes along the Pacific coast of Salmon Nation vary from year to year but have surpassed 300,000 in some recent counts. They are usually found in small groups in more populated areas but sometimes occur in numbers of up to five hundred. These cultural traditions and the animals themselves are at risk.

Northern fur seal *(Callorhinus ursinus).* Formerly abundant at the northern edge of Salmon Nation in the Pribilof Islands, this fur seal has dense fur over most of its body but large, bare flippers. Mature bulls reach weights of up to six hundred pounds, and historically were targeted for commercial harvesting by Russian and American trading companies, which employed indigenous hunters. Over two and a half million individuals were harvested between 1786 and 1867, dramatically depleting the populations. In 1869, the U.S. began to protect the Pribilof Island populations from hunting, but the northern fur seal reached its known population ebb in 1912, when only 216,000 were left. Populations have recovered enough to allow small-scale subsistence hunting by indigenous peoples but have declined since the 1970s. Culturally at risk.

Ringed seal *(Phoca hispida)*. This seal has historically served the northernmost coastal peoples of Salmon Nation as their most abundant and reliable source of meat. In Alaska through western and central Canada, they come within reach of hunters with the springtime thaw. The colorful technique of "breathing hole hunting" formerly required harpooners to stay still, in waiting, at the edge of a seal's breathing hole for hours on end. Heavy caliber rifles are now used but are not necessarily more efficient. Seal netting has declined even more than traditional harpooning. Except for winter ice-edge sealing, these ancient hunting techniques are at risk as cultural traditions.

Steller's or **Northern sea lion** *(Eumetopias jubatus)*. Larger and lighter in color than California sea lions, Steller's range from the Bering Strait to California. For centuries, they were harvested by subsistence hunters but were then decimated in the twentieth century by fish farmers attempting to protect their stocks. The current population of Steller's sea lions is about 40,000, down from 197,000 in 1967. There is great concern

Steller's sea lion

about this population, which has dropped by 80 percent since the 1970s. In 1997, one northwestern Alaska population of Steller's was listed as endangered, while the rest remained listed as threatened in the U.S. and Canada. Reasons for declines vary by place. However, researchers believe that a decline in the abundance of fish they eat is the strongest factor. Drowning, entanglement in nets, pests, diseases, and overhunting are other causes for the Steller's decline. The species remains protected under the Endangered Species Act and the Marine Mammal Protection Act, forbidding the killing, harming, or harassing of any marine mammal. There is hope for the recovery of Steller's sea lion populations if efforts to reopen hunting are controlled. Endangered.

Steller's sea cow *(Hydrodamalis gigas)*. This marine mammal, related to manatees, is now extinct. From the time it was first seen by Europeans, the small population of Steller's sea cows was restricted to Arctic water around Bering and Copper islands. There, males of this species reached lengths of twenty-five feet, and weighed more than the largest male walruses. They were distinguished from large seals by their two stout forelimbs and a whalelike tail. Perhaps never numbering more than a few thousand individuals, this small population was rapidly extirpated once sailors, seal hunters, and fur traders began to follow Bering's route past Copper Island to Alaska. Steller's sea cows were voraciously pursued by seafarering hunters for their meat, fat, and skins and their populations dramatically declined. Hardly a quarter century after Steller offered the first scientific description of this sea cow, the species had been driven to extinction.

Walrus

Walrus *(Odobenus rosmarus).* Available but dangerous as prey for indigenous hunters off the northwest Alaska coast throughout the summer, these predatory marine mammals congregate where seals are also abundant. From July on, walrus herds are approached by crews of kayakers with heavy rifles, while other crews work on land nearby to butcher the animals. The meat, the heart, and even some of the skin were traditionally boiled together in pots of water. Alaska Natives in Wainwright are among the many traditional hunters now concerned about the excessive slaughter and wasting of walruses by less experienced hunters. In the western Bering Sea, Pacific walrus populations are severely depleted. Many factors that affect what fish the walruses eat may be contributing to their declines, including high levels of illegal fishing in the western Bering Sea, overfishing of particular fisheries, and the taking of nontarget species, or bycatch. Global warming is an impending risk. Threatened as a cultural tradition.

WHALE

Gray whale

Gray whale *(Eschrichtius gibbosus).* Historically called the "devil fish" for its feistiness, this migratory species was nearly brought to extinction by commercial whaling before it was protected by international treaty agreements in the 1940s. The populations that approach the coasts of Salmon Nation now exceed twenty thousand individuals, and are no longer listed as threatened or endangered. Certain indigenous peoples have engaged in subsistence hunting of whales for thousands of years. Subsistence hunting differs from commercial hunting in that the whales are consumed in the locale where they are caught, rather than sold. There has been much debate in recent years regarding the rights of subsistence hunters to harvest whale species that have long been part of their food traditions, when the animals have suffered historic declines. Many observers point out that subsistence whaling such as that which the Inuit have practiced has not been a major cause of these declines, and so the International Whaling Commission has allowed some exceptions to its general ban on gray whale hunting, recognizing that there are issues of cultural as well as biological survival embedded in this issue.

Beluga or **White whale** *(Delphinapterus leucas).* Twelve to sixteen feet long and weighing about three thousand pounds per individual, the pure white belugas

travel in large pods. They arrive along the Alaskan and Canadian coasts as early as March, well before large whales migrate through. They were traditionally hunted from skin-covered kayaks with harpoon and later, with rifles. The prized meat from a single hunt historically could feed a family for up to two years. Hunting is certainly the main cause of the dramatic recent declines in beluga populations. However, the damming of rivers, noise pollution from ships, dredging, and industrial environmental pollution have resulted in declines in the beluga's habitat quality and

Beluga whale

food supply. While already endangered in the Atlantic, they are at a lower level of risk in the Pacific.

WILD BERRIES AND NUTS

BARBERRY

Cascade Oregon grape *(Mahonia nervosa)*. One of several species of Oregon grape, this shrub has fat, juicy, dark-blue berries with a silvery bloom on their skin, resembling miniature grapes. It grows in coastal mountains from California to British Columbia, favoring the light shade of the Cascades' coniferous forests. Lewis and Clark found it at Celilo Falls in 1805, and it was then described scientifically, although Native Americans such as the Skagit had used this sour berry for centuries prior to that, often mashing and mixing them with salal or huckleberries to make sweet berry cakes. Many contemporary residents of Salmon Nation use them for jams and jellies, marketing them in California, Oregon, and Washington. Not at risk.

Cascade Oregon grape

Tall Oregon grape *(Mahonia aquifolium)*. This species is taller and has fewer leaflets on its leaves than the Cascade species but offers tart, bluish purple berries in midsummer. Growing from British Columbia south to California, from the Pacific coast to Idaho, it thrives on the edges of woods, along rocky slopes, and in clearings. It is the state flower of Oregon. Its berries were eaten fresh, mashed, or dried and stored by many First Peoples; immigrants used them for wine, jam, drinks, and desserts, and used other parts of the plants as medicine. Oregon grape juice of either species makes an excellent jelly, alone or in combination with juice of salal, rosehips, or blackberries. This species was introduced to Europe by David Douglas and is widely grown as a fruit and ornamental. Common, and not at risk.

BLACKBERRY AND RASPBERRY

Arctic raspberry, Plumboy, or **Naigoonberry** *(Rubus arcticus)*. A short, nonprickly plant with many flowering shoots, the Arctic raspberry grows in muskegs and on creek banks across Alaska and Canada. The berries are so fragrant and delicious that many peoples consider it the most excellent of all wild fruits within their homelands. Though it is not picked as much as formerly, it is not at risk.

Cloudberry

Cloudberry, Baked-apple, Malt-berry, Mars apple, or **Fox berry** *(Rubus chamaemorus)*. This low, creeping perennial grows in muskegs and peat bogs but does not fruit in all habitats. It grows only in moist acidic soils, and has a wide geographic range in Canada and the northwestern U.S. Somewhat sour in taste, the soft, yellowish fruits are juicy when ripe and relished by deer and humans alike. The Haida and Tsimshian historically harvested huge quantities in midsummer, storing them in water or freezing them. The Masset Co-op Store formerly sold canned "Mars Apples" for $1.25 per pound. These plants are rarely even found in fruit anymore. While Haida and Tsimshian elders remember them fondly, many youth among coastal tribes have never even harvested or tasted them. Endangered as a cultural tradition.

Wild raspberry *(Rubus idaeus)*. The same species as domesticated raspberry, this wild shrub is short and prickly. Its red (or rarely yellow) berries are smaller and sweeter than domesticated raspberry varieties, and are widespread in the interior of Salmon Nation. There, they remain widely used; they are eaten fresh, jellied, or frozen for later use. Their yields are enhanced by burning and some forms of logging. Although not as productive as formerly, it is not at risk.

Blackcap raspberry

Blackcap raspberry or **Black raspberry** *(Rubus leucodermis)*. These dark-purple (or rarely yellow) berries fall off their prickly shrubs when ripe. They vary from sweet and juicy to bland, watery, and seedy, but at least one dozen aboriginal peoples ate them fresh, or dried them into cakes stored in maple bark baskets or bags. Elders of First Nations claim that it grows better after burning (or selective logging). Although still very popular, they are not as common as a century ago because of fire suppression, and are in decline enough to be considered at risk.

Thimbleberry *(Rubus parviflorus).* This erect, many stemmed, thornless bush produces numerous delicate ruby-red berries that are the size and shape of sewing thimbles. It grows in open forests and along stream banks throughout Salmon Nation. The berries were historically harvested in quantities to eat fresh with fish, since the ripe ones are so tender and perishable. Different stands have different flavors and textures. The green tender shoots are also peeled and eaten and the large, soft leaves are used for drying berries on, or in pit-cooking. It has an extensive range along the Pacific coast, and favors open habitats, including roadsides and logged areas. Not at risk.

Salmonberry *(Rubus spectabilis).* A taller shrub than its other raspberry kin, this prickly plant prefers shaded swamps and moist clearings. Its geographic range along the coast stretches from Alaska through Oregon. The ripened berries come in different colors—golden, ruby, and dark purple. The green, tender shoots are also peeled and eaten. Coastal-dwelling natives and immigrants still harvest enormous quantities for fresh local use. Not at risk.

Salmonberry

Trailing wild blackberry *(Rubus ursinus).* A low-trailing perennial of the Pacific coast, this early fruiting shrub is found in moist forests from timberline down to sea level. It extends from southern British Columbia into western Washington and Oregon. According to legend, the blood of a First Nations woman was transformed into the vine that bears these berries. While many of its harvesters favor its excellent flavor to that of the introduced Himalayan Blackberry *(Rubus discolor),* the latter has eclipsed it in use due to greater ease of picking. Its cultural use may also be in decline because the plant is adapted to frequent burning, and fire suppression is reducing its productivity. The leaves, especially the reddish colored winter leaves, are used as a beverage tea and to sweeten medicinal teas made from tree barks. At risk as a tradition.

BLUEBERRY AND HUCKLEBERRY

Alaska blueberry *(Vaccinium alaskaense).* These large bluish or reddish black berries are few-seeded and stand erect on the deciduous branches of a shrub that lives in moist coniferous forests and along boggy shores of streams. From Alaska through Washington, virtually all coastal peoples ate this rather acidic, watery blueberry dried, fresh, or frozen. It is still canned or frozen by First Nations peoples, who also make it into jam. Although it is not picked as much as formerly, often being supplanted by commercially available blueberries, it remains common and is not at risk.

Dwarf mountain blueberry

Dwarf mountain blueberry *(Vaccinium caespitosum)*. These berries develop close to the ground on very small, low bushes. However, the berries are large and were formerly picked in quantity and dried throughout western Washington and in some places in British Columbia. They are now frozen or made into jam. Although not threatened biologically, it is at risk as a cultural tradition.

Cascade bilberry

Cascade bilberry or **Cascade huckleberry** *(Vaccinium deliciosum)*. This delicious, sweet-tasting berry grows on low bushes in the Cascades of Washington and British Columbia. They are large and blue. Sometimes harvesters claim that they have the smell and aftertaste of pine pitch. At risk as a cultural tradition, even though the plant itself is common.

Black mountain huckleberry, Black blueberry, or **Bilberry** *(Vaccinium membranaceum)*. These large, exceedingly sweet, shiny berries were called "the head of all fruits" by the Nlaka'pmx (Thompson) Indians. Eaten fresh or dried into cakes, this was the most important and popular of all the berry species in Washington and British Columbia, where several different varieties were named in various languages. Their growth is enhanced by periodic fire, so berry patches that are not burned or tended decline in vigor. It remains featured in First Fruits ceremonies at Warm Springs and elsewhere; large quantities continue to be harvested and sold for as much as eighteen dollars per quart. However, there are reports of increased competition, and of diminishing size and abundance possibly due to fire suppression. As a cultural tradition, it is clearly threatened by competitive commercial harvesting.

Canada blueberry

Canada, Sourtop, or **Velvet-leaf blueberry** *(Vaccinium myrtilloides)*. These sweet, easy-to-harvest berries grow on low bushes in dense patches in both British Columbia and Washington. They were formerly picked in quantity and dried, or made into excellent pies. They are now frozen or made into jam. Although not threatened biologically, its cultural traditions are at risk, as few people pick it in any quantity anymore.

Bog or **Moss cranberry** *(Vaccinium oxycoccus).* This slender, creeping vine produces both round and elongated berries that stay green and hard for weeks before turning red in late autumn. Tasting like commercial cranberries, they grow in peat bogs, especially around sphagnum moss, or wherever bogs are found in Salmon Nation. Most coastal peoples would historically journey to bogs and muskegs to harvest them, storing them in damp moss underwater. Immigrants purchased them from First Nations harvesters only if they were red and soft. Much of their habitat has been drained or fragmented near cities, but the food is not globally threatened. At risk.

Evergreen, Shot, or **Black winter huckleberry** *(Vaccinium ovatum).*

Evergreen huckleberry

These small, tart berries come in different colors, from glistening black to powdery blue. They are locally abundant but sporadic in coastal old-growth forests or on salt-sprayed beaches from Alaska through central California. Ripening late compared to other berries, they are harvested and eaten raw from autumn through

Keeping It Wild

I remember the thrills of catching my first coho salmon, eating my first mouthful of salmonberries, and harvesting my first bunch of lobster mushrooms from a spruce-covered slope in the Cascades. I can also recall the puzzlement on the face of my four-year-old son when he got his first peek at a bucket full of geoducks harvested by his uncle not far from Semiahmoo Point near the Washington border with British Columbia. "Ooooh, Papa, look at that! Those gooey ducks are all boys!"

What is it about these foods, and the foraging of them, that gives us so much pleasure? It may well be that it is the deep connection they offer us with wild places. Their flavors, textures, colors, and shapes speak the word "wild" to us whenever we encounter them, and that is simply something we do not gain from domesticated grains or pastured livestock.

That is why it is unsettling to hear that research laboratories around the world have been genetically manipulating coho and chinook salmon; rainbow and cutthroat trout; Arctic char and flounder; oysters and even abalone! Most of what is called "wild rice" in the U.S. marketplace is grown under irrigation in central California, using seed stocks selected and manipulated by our own land-grant colleges, undermining the traditions of First Nations cultures that rely entirely on truly "wild" rice.

Whether it be farmed Atlantic salmon, or genetically manipulated rice, these foods simply don't have the truly wild flavors and textures that many of us hope and pray for. Both their authenticity and their ultimate sustainability should be questioned.

As Winona La Duke has suggested, there is a clear alternative to accepting these façades: "Keep it wild!" When we vote with our mouths, bellies, and wallets for the truly wild, traditionally harvested, sustainably produced heritage foods of our region, we are supporting the survival not only of the species itself, but its natural habitats and the community stewards that care for them.

Gary Paul Nabhan is the founder of the RAFT consortium, Director of the Center for Sustainable Environments, and author of Coming Home to Eat.

winter; their leaves are also used as floral greens. They may be stored fresh, frozen, or made into jam. Northwest tribes within reach have harvested vast quantities of berries, which they formed into cakes to dry on roofs and platforms. This slow growing species does not compete well against aggressive understory species, so may be declining in areas of industrial rotational logging. Commonly propagated in at least twenty nurseries, it is vulnerable in the wild to inappropriate forest management practices. It is clearly at risk as a tradition.

Oval-leaved or **Gray blueberry** *(Vaccinium ovalifolium)*. This sweet tasting, singly borne berry is light blue, and fruits early on medium-sized bushes that have oval leaves. Because it is one of the first berries to ripen at the end of winter, it remains very popular, and is still used in British Columbia and Washington. Found along forest edges, it was formerly picked in quantity and dried, but it is now frozen or made into jam. It is at risk as a cultural tradition because few people pick it in quantity anymore.

Red or **Deciduous huckleberry** *(Vaccinium parvifolium)*. These bright red berries are tart and tangy, sweet and flavorful. They ripen in August and September from Alaska to Washington. This species favors young coastal forests and thinned stands more than the evergreen huckleberries do. Now used in pies and jellies, some Northwest tribes formerly had one of their first fruit celebrations coincide with its harvest. Formerly picked in quantity and dried, the berries are now frozen or made into jam. Their populations are enhanced by clearing and burning but are in decline where these practices no longer occur. Its traditions are at risk.

Red huckleberry

Grouseberry or **Red whortleberry** *(Vaccinium scoparium)*. This bush lies low, with small leaves, and tiny red berries that remind First Nations peoples of salmon eggs. It inhabits subalpine forests in British Columbia, and has a more restricted range than other berries. Because it is very hard to pick, its use is in decline, and its traditions are at risk.

Bog blueberry or **Bog whortleberry** *(Vaccinium uliginosum)*. This low, spreading bush has bluish leaves and berries that have a waxy coating. The large, sweet

Lingonberry

berries were harvested from bogs and muskegs near the Pacific coast far more in the past than in the present. Because they are little used today among the dozen tribes that formerly coveted them, their cultural traditions are threatened.

Lingonberry or **Lowbush cranberry** *(Vaccinium vitis-idaea)*. This low evergreen, matlike bush harbors bright red berries that are soft and clustered. They are tart but late-ripening in the bogs, rocky barrens, and forested cliffs that they inhabit in British Columbia. They were formerly stored underwater for later use but not dried. While not threatened biologically, their cultural traditions are nevertheless at risk.

BUNCHBERRY AND DOGWOOD

Red-osier dogwood *(Cornus sericea).* This shrub has white, quite bitter berries with hard-seeded drupes. It was formerly eaten by the Interior people of Salmon Nation as a mouth freshener and in mixtures with Saskatoon berries. Widespread, not at risk.

Bunchberry *(Cornus canadensis).* This species produces clusters of red, aggregatelike drupes that can be mildly sweet or bland; they have been used in puddings, jams, and sauces and are mixed with other berries. While some tribes ate the berries fresh, others avoided them. This species is widespread in moist coastal and subalpine forests, occurring in all states and provinces of the Northwest, from sea level to eight thousand feet. Its cultural traditions are at risk, since few people pick them anymore.

Bunchberry

HIGHBUSH CRANBERRY

Highbush cranberry *(Viburnum edule).* Round, shiny, red-orange berries are picked off this straggly shrub in late summer or fall, or sometimes even in midwinter when frozen. They are hard and extremely acidic unless stored underwater to after-ripen; then they become soft and tart. Historically, they were served with crabapples and whipped eulachon grease. They range from sea level to subalpine forests above the coast, across much of Salmon Nation. Although not threatened biologically, their associated traditions are at risk as harvest has declined.

Highbush cranberry

Highbush *(Viburnum opulus).* Similar to the above species, this one occurs in the interior of Salmon Nation, where elite families used to "own and manage" particular gathering grounds. It was once harvested in quantity but is not as common today, perhaps due to livestock grazing and habitat destruction. Its cultural traditions are clearly threatened.

HAZELNUT (FILBERT)

Beaked hazelnut *(Corylus cornuta).* A tasty nut over one half-inch long but with very bristly husks, this wild variety is distinct from the Eastern filbert and resistant

Beaked hazelnut

to its blight. It grows wild from British Columbia to northern California but is also available for planting from Burnt Ridge and Forestfarm Nursery. It is common in the wild but rare in trade. It is a shrub that was historically tended by burning and pruning; it is now said to be much less productive than formerly, and thus little used. Because it has mostly been replaced by commercial nuts, its wild-harvesting traditions are now at risk.

CURRANT AND GOOSEBERRY

Gray currant *(Ribes bracteosum)*. This smooth-stemmed shrub has large, musky leaves and powdery blue or gray berries that grow on

Gray currant

long leader stalks, making them easy to pick. They are found on the water's edge around lakes and creeks, and in wetlands made by avalanche clearings at higher elevations in Salmon Nation. They are eaten raw and used in mixed-fruit salads or for jams. Formerly they were dried for storage, often mixed with salal berries. Once widely eaten, they are barely used today, perhaps due to their resinous aftertaste. Threatened as a tradition because few people pick them in quantity anymore.

Coastal black gooseberry

Coastal black or **Straggly gooseberry** *(Ribes divaricatum)*. Found on shrubs that may either be erect or spreading, this gooseberry has excellent flavor. It is grape-green when unripe but becomes purplish black and almost translucent, with a tangy flavor when fully ripened. The berries, which ripen over a long time frame, are difficult to gather in quantity. Growing along the coastline in open woods and clearings, this shrub is common west of the Cascades in Washington, Oregon, and British Columbia. All coastal cultures gathered them, and many boiled and mixed them with ooligan grease for special berry feasts. Formerly enhanced by burning, they are no longer as productive. Not biologically threatened but at risk as a cultural tradition because their harvesting has declined.

Sticky or **Pioneer gooseberry** *(Ribes lobbii)*. This stout, branching shrub produces large purplish berries with sticky hairs that may be spherical or elongated. Although now very rare on Vancouver Island, it was formerly common there and often used historically. It may have been removed by foresters because it is an alternate host to white-pine blister rust. No longer eaten as part of Vancouver Island traditions, the species persists in Washington, Oregon, and northern California. Their use is threatened as a cultural tradition, as few pick them in quantity anymore.

MOUNTAIN-ASH

Sitka mountain-ash *(Sorbus sitchensis)*. A low tree with soft, red-orange berries that contain very tart, yellow flesh. Only a few First Nations peoples relish this food plant, while others believe it is poisonous. Found from Alaska to California in three provinces and six states, it is biologically common but more or less restricted to Salmon Nation. Where used, it was mixed with blueberries or made into a marinade for marmot and other meats. It is little used today, and is definitely a cultural tradition at risk.

Sitka mountain-ash

PLUM AND CHERRY

Klamath or **Sierra plum** *(Prunus subcordata)*. A wild plum of the Sierras, its inch-diameter yellow and red fruit are famous for wild plum preserves. They may be similar to or even the same as the Potawatomi Plum of the Colorado Plateau and Great Basin. A native shrub restricted to California and Oregon, the Klamath plum is available as seed only from Callahan Seeds in Central Point, Oregon and as nursery stock only from Forestfarm Nursery in Williams, Oregon. Rare but recovering.

Choke cherry *(Prunus virginiana)*. This wild cherry occurs across North America, but in the Northwest, at least, there are several different forms, ranging in color from translucent red to deep, blackish purple. The red-colored ones are said to be sweeter and less "puckery" than the darker fruits. Choke cherry were a staple fruit for First Nations throughout their range in the Interior Plateau of British Columbia north to the Yukon and south to California. While not gathered to the same extent as formerly, it is not at risk.

Choke cherry

Bird cherry or **Oso berry** *(Oemleria cerasiformis)*. This tall, dioecious shrub produces clusters of large-seeded plums, small and thin-fleshed but sweet. Very early in ripening, they are yellowish red while maturing but turn dark blue and drop off the bushes very quickly when ripe. They grow in moist open woods from British Columbia through northern California, and were eaten by several tribes, fresh or dried. Restricted in range but common in places, this species is not biologically threatened. Its cultural traditions are at risk due to declines in harvesting.

Bird cherry

ROSE

Wood's rose

Rosehips, from **Dwarf** *(Rosa gymnocarpa);* **Nootka** *(Rosa nutkana);* **Prickly** *(Rosa acicularis);* **Swamp** *(Rosa pisocarpa);* and **Wood's** *(Rosa woodsii).* All the wild roses have edible hips, but the seeds need to be removed or the fruits strained before use because of small, irritating hairs. They are all good for jelly and for tea. Rose hips are well-known for their rich vitamin C content. The young shoots can also be peeled and eaten. The hips of *R. nutkana* and *R. acicularis* are particularly productive and good tasting. Although none are biologically threatened in Salmon Nation, they are at risk as parts of nearly forgotten immigrant and indigenous traditions.

SERVICEBERRY

Pale serviceberry *(Amelanchier pallida).* A short, shrubby species, the pale serviceberry has a reddish purple fruit with a pleasant flavor. This species occurs from coastal ranges to the Sierras in five states but not in Canada, and in damp meadows and sparse thickets. Because it can colonize roadsides and clearings, it is not at risk.

Saskatoon berry *(Amelanchier alnifolia).* This species produces fruit up to one half-inch in diameter; they turn dull red, then purple, and then add a misty bluish bloom. They are variable in taste and size, seediness, and juiciness. The berries were formerly dried in large quantities and used in preparation of many different dishes. They were known for their sweetness and were used to sweeten other fruits. Occurring from sea level to subalpine talus slopes from Alaska south into many states and provinces, the Saskatoon cultural traditions were most strongly developed in Salmon Nation. It was the most important of the fruits for Interior peoples, who recognized several named varieties in their native languages. A commercial Saskatoon farm has been established on Vancouver Island. This species is put somewhat at risk by habitat degradation and vegetation changes, and is no longer used as much.

SALAL

Salal

Salal *(Gaultheria shallon).* Salal's seedy, dark-purple berries grow on one-sided stems, and are set on a spreading evergreen shrub that forms dense thickets. Common from the eastern base of the Cascades and Sierras to the Pacific coast, it extends from California through British Columbia. The most important of the berries in the coastal parts

of Salmon Nation, it was a staple for centuries, dipped in whale or seal oil, or mashed and dried into cakes for storage in cedar boxes. The berries vary in flavor depending on habitat and ripening conditions, but the best ones are sweet and juicy. They make excellent jams and jellies, particularly when mixed with Oregon grape berries. The ceremonial uses and elaborate storage traditions have declined, but salal berries are still commonly picked in many areas. The leafy branches are pruned for a commercial harvest as floral greens and shipped all around the world. This is a concern for some First Nations peoples who fear that this will impair their fruit production. Salal may possibly be at risk as a cultural tradition in places where fewer people pick them in quantity.

CREEPING SNOWBERRY

Creeping snowberry *(Chiogenes hispidula).* These small, wintergreen flavored berries are very sweet and were traditionally used for tea. The species has a very limited distribution in peatbogs of central British Columbia, and does not reach into the U.S. It is little known or used today and its habitat is being reduced by development, putting its traditions at risk.

Creeping snowberry

SOAPBERRY

Soopolallie, Russet, or **Cascade buffaloberry** *(Shepherdia canadensis).* These reddish orange to (rarely) yellow, translucent berries are produced by this dioecious shrub of dry, open forest habitats. It prefers openings along streams, from Alaska to Oregon and eastward into Montana. The berries were historically harvested by placing mats or baskets underneath the spreading shrubs and striking their branches with sticks,

Soopolallie

causing the ripe berries to fall off. The fruits were then mixed with water and sweeteners to be whipped into a very light salmon-colored froth, called "Indian ice cream." This highly valued dessert is still featured at tribal feasts throughout Salmon Nation, and people also drink a lemonadelike beverage made from the fruits. The berries were historically used as a potlatch gift and a trade item between tribes in Alaska and British Columbia. They are still a valued gift. They are sporadic in their productivity and are not used as much as formerly. Many people who would like to use them are not able to find them in quantity, since they were formerly tended and maintained by fire. At risk culturally.

STRAWBERRY

Seaside strawberry

Seaside strawberry *(Fragaria chiloensis)*. A juicy and divinely delicious strawberry growing to marble-size in some places, this species grows only in sand or on rocky crevices along the Pacific coast, from California through British Columbia. Of the three strawberry species in Salmon Nation, its range is the most restricted—to shorelines, sand dunes, and coastal bluffs. It was historically hybridized with other wild species to produce the domesticated strawberry that graces most tables in the temperate world. The seaside strawberries at Naikoon, on the north coast of Graham Island, Haida Gwaii (Queen Charlotte Islands), are particularly famous for their size and flavor. Although they remain very popular among most coastal peoples, some say that they are no longer as common, and several historically known California populations are extirpated. Those remaining are largely endangered by habitat loss.

WALNUT

California black, Hinds, or **Claro walnut** *(Juglans hindsii)*. A large black walnut from a semicultivated strain of the Hinds or Claro, it has a delicious, high quality nut. It is found on lighter, human disturbed soils encircling California Indian settlements, where it once grew fifty feet tall, providing an abundant fall harvest for winter storage. Although once available from at least ten nurseries for planting, seven now maintain it. Threatened.

WILD GAME

Black bear

Black bear *(Ursus americanus)*. Creatures of northern forests and adjacent muskegs, black bears are stout, short-legged, and fast-running animals, widely respected for their mythically awesome personages. They are omnivorous, with a diet that shifts dramatically between seasons. Their meat is considered a spiritual delicacy and a nourishing food. A bear feast is held in certain indigenous communities, and the most valuable meat from black bears is reserved for community potlatch feasts. Although there remain high numbers of black bears in many places within Alaska and adjacent territories, conflicts are increasing between bears and humans wherever new developments encroach on their habitats. Some cultural traditions are therefore at risk.

Cascade moose *(Alces alces).* A resident of northern forests and shallow wetlands, this relatively small black moose is limited in range within the U.S. to the northern Cascades and some outlier habitat near Spokane, Washington. Populations of other moose subspecies become more common in Canada and Alaska. The meat of all subspecies is rich and delicious, and is savored whether dried, boiled, roasted, or fried. The Cascade moose is at risk in southern Salmon Nation, but other subspecies with wider ranges have also declined in numbers since the 1960s.

Cascade moose

Black-tailed deer *(Odocoileus hemionus* spp.) These small but beautiful deer with antlers in forked pairs have dark tails and light faces and muzzles. The weight of the bucks ranges from one hundred to two hundred pounds. The Oregon subspecies is known to a few areas of Oregon, Washington, and a broader area of British Columbia, while the Sitka subspecies is in coastal Alaska, including several islands. In the Sitka area, it has long been prized as meat by Tlingit, Russian, and Anglo inhabitants of the coastal rainforests. It is still celebrated there, as the writings of

Black-tailed deer

Richard Nelson attest. In Oregon and Washington, its history is more obscure, but it is now suffering from a hair loss disease that has afflicted it for more than a decade. Its dependence on old-growth forests has put it in peril in British Columbia, Washington, Oregon, and in parts of the Tongass in Alaska. At risk in Oregon and Washington but in greater health and abundance to the north.

Columbian white-tailed deer *(Odocoileus virginianus leucurus).* A medium-sized deer with a cinnamon-brown coat and a triangular tail that exposes snow-white fur when flashed, this is the westernmost white-tailed subspecies. Tens of thousands were historically found in tidal spruce forests of the Willamette, Columbia, and Umpqua River valleys. The Columbian white-tailed deer population has suffered both from loss of habitat and overhunting. In the early 1900s, the total population size hovered between two hundred and four hundred individuals, until regulations aided in its recovery. Nevertheless, the clearing of floodplain forests for fields and pastures has dramatically reduced the availability of unfragmented riparian habitat required by this species. Disease problems continue to plague it. Endangered.

Dall sheep

Dall or **Thinhorn sheep** *(Ovis dalli).* This rugged mountain climbing "goat" inhabits alpine and Arctic tundra in the uplands of Alaska, the Yukon, and British Columbia. Kin to musk ox and bighorn, these sheep can have either snowy white, gray, or black coats of short wool, depending on the subspecies. Rams can weigh up to 250 pounds. Not currently at risk.

Mountain beaver *(Aplodonta rufa).* First scientifically described by Lewis and Clark in 1806, the mountain beaver is not merely a fur bearer but also a prized source of meat. For the Koyukon Athapaskans, beaver meat is savored among the best food the northern forest provides. Roasted, boiled, dried, or smoked, beaver tail meat, liver, and kidneys remain delicacies. This habitat-modifying keystone species of streams and wetlands frequents both riparian and coniferous woodlands for its dam-building materials. Under its reddish brown fur is one to three pounds of meat, which is flavorful provided that fatty scent glands have been carefully removed before cooking. They were harvested from ponds and river deadfalls in the spring, and the meat was sometimes smoked. Fur trapping and river damming in the nineteenth century wiped out many populations, some of which have since returned. Recovering but still vulnerable.

Mountain goat *(Oreamnos americanus).* From Alaska's most remote ranges southward, the mountain goat is the signature game species of alpine summits and craggy ridge crests. It is pursued by subsistence and sport hunters alike, with conflicts not uncommon between the two groups. There remain many remote populations that are not yet at risk in any way.

Mountain goat

Roosevelt or **Olympic elk** *(Cervus elaphus roosevelti).* These towering herbivores inhabit Pacific coastal forests from northern California and Oregon, northward into Washington and Vancouver Island of British Columbia. Their meat becomes flavored by their relish of huckleberry, trailing wild blackberry, vine maple, and salal in late summer and fall through early winter. From late winter through early summer, they survive on standing crops of grasses and herbs. This subspecies is at risk.

Woodland caribou

Woodland caribou *(Rangifer tarandus caribou).* Found from Idaho, Montana, and Washington northward into much of western Canada and Alaska, this migratory herding species has been extremely important to many cultures, including the Athapaskans of Alaska and the Yukon. The caribou that become fattened by spring foraging are favored as food. Several dried and smoked caribou meat products are available through the Internet from Native American sources. The caribou is protected from hunting in states such as Idaho. Threatened biologically and at risk as a cultural tradition.

COMMON NAME	SCIENTIFIC NAME	SUPPLIERS
Alaska blueberry	*Vaccinium alaskaense*	Landscape Alaska, Streamside Native Plants
Arctic raspberry, Plumboy, or Naigoonberry	*Rubis arcticus*	One Green World, Danamac Acres
Beaked hazelnut	*Corylus cornuta*	Burnt Ridge Nursery, Streamside Native Plants
Bing cherry	*Prunus avium*	Trees of Antiquity, Forestfarm Nursery
Bird cherry or Oso berry	*Oemleria cerasiformis*	Forestfarm Nursery, One Green World, Streamside Native Plants
Black mountain huckleberry, Black blueberry, or Bilberry	*Vaccinium membranaceum*	Streamside Native Plants
Black Republican cherry	*Prunus avium*	C&O Nursery
Blackcap or Black raspberry	*Rubus leucodermis*	Raintree Nursery
Blenheim apricot	*Prunus armeniaca*	Trees of Antiquity
Bog blueberry or Bog whortleberry	*Vaccinium uliginosum*	Streamside Native Plants
Bog or Moss cranberry	*Vaccinium oxycoccus*	Forestfarm Nursery, Gardens North
Bunchberry	*Cornus canadensis*	Fritz Creek Gardens, Kenaitze Greenhouse & Gardens, Streamside Native Plants
Butter clam	*Saxidomus giganteus*	Anacortes Aquaculture LLC, Brenner Oyster Co.
California black, Hinds, or Claro walnut	*Juglans hindsii*	Freshwater Farms
Canada, Sourtop, or Velvet-leaf blueberry	*Vaccinium myrtilloides*	Gardens North
Cascade bilberry or Cascade huckleberry	*Vaccinium deliciosum*	Wallace W. Hansen Native Plants of the Northwest Native Plant Nursery & Gardens
Cascade Oregon grape	*Mahonia nervosa*	One Green World, Forestfarm Nursery, Streamside Native Plants
Charlotte peach	*Prunus persica*	One Green World
Choke cherry	*Prunus virginiana*	Forestfarm Nursery, Methow Native Nursery, Freshwater Farms
Cloudberry, Baked-apple, Malt-berry, Mars apple, or Fox berry	*Rubus chamaemorus*	Pacific Rim Native Plant Nursery
Coastal black or Straggly gooseberry	*Ribes divaricatum*	Wallace W. Hansen Native Plants of the Northwest Native Plant Nursery & Gardens

COMMON NAME	SCIENTIFIC NAME	SUPPLIERS
Creeping snowberry	*Chiogenes hispidula*	Gardens North
Dungeness crab	*Cancer magister*	Quinault Pride Seafood
Dwarf mountain blueberry	*Vaccinium caespitosum*	Wallace W. Hansen Native Plants of the Northwest Native Plant Nursery & Gardens
Evergreen, Shot, or Black winter huckleberry	*Vaccinium ovatum*	One Green World, Forestfarm Nursery, Larner Seeds, Streamside Native Plants
Red abalone	*Haliotis rufescens*	U.S. Abalone Farm
Geoduck	*Panopea abrupta*	Taylor Shellfish Farms, Inc., Lummi Hatchery, Whiskey Creek Shellfish, Alutiiq Pride Shellfish Hatchery, Hama Hama Company
Gillette fig	*Ficus carica*	Oregon Exotics Rare Fruit Nursery
Gramma Walters bean	*Phaseolus vulgaris*	Abundant Life Seeds, Seed and Plant Sanctuary for Canada
Gray currant	*Ribes bracteosum*	Streamside Native Plants
Grouseberry or Red whortleberry	*Vaccinium scoparium*	Wallace W. Hansen Native Plants of the Northwest Native Plant Nursery & Gardens
Hamma Hamma oyster	*Crassostrea gigas*	Taylor Shellfish Farms, Inc., Hama Hama Company
Heart cockle	*Clinocardium nuttallii*	Alutiiq Pride Shellfish Hatchery, Anacortes Aquaculture LLC
Highbush	*Viburnum opulus*	Forestfarm Nursery
Highbush cranberry	*Viburnum edule*	One Green World, Forestfarm Nursery, Streamside Native Plants
Hood strawberry	*Fragaria X ananassa*	One Green World, Fruit-tree.com Nursery
Hooker's Sweet Indian corn	*Zea mays*	Seeds of Change
Hudson's golden gem apple	*Malus X domestica*	One Green World, Trees of Antiquity
Immigrant bean	*Phaseolus vulgaris*	Seed and Plant Sanctuary for Canada
Inchelium Red garlic	*Allium sativum* var. *sativum*	Seeds of Change, Seed Savers Exchange
Introduced "Japanese" oyster	*Crassostrea gigas*	Taylor Shellfish Farms, Inc.
Kilham goose bean	*Phaseolus vulgaris*	Abundant Life Seeds
Klamath or Sierra plum	*Prunus subcordata*	Forestfarm Nursery, Callahan Seeds
Lambert cherry	*Prunus avium*	Fruit-tree.com Nursery
Lingonberry or Lowbush cranberry	*Vaccinium vitis-idaea*	Forestfarm Nursery, Burnt Ridge Nursery, Kenaitze Greenhouse & Gardens

COMMON NAME	SCIENTIFIC NAME	SUPPLIERS
Littleneck clam	*Protothaca staminea*	Coast Seafoods, Taylor Shellfish, Whiskey Creek Shellfish Hatchery, Lummi Hatchery, Alutiiq Pride Shellfish Hatchery, Hama Hama Company
Loganberry	*Rubus ursinus* var. *loganobaccus*	Trees of Antiquity, One Green World
Lorz Italian garlic	*Allium sativum* var. *sativum*	Seed Savers Exchange
Lower Salmon River squash	*Cucurbita maxima*	Seed Savers Exchange member Steve Ford, Maine Organic Farmers and Gardeners Association
Lucas navy bean	*Phaseolus vulgaris*	Abundant Life Seeds
Marshall strawberry	*Fragraria X ananassa*	USDA/Agricultural Research Service National Clonal Germplasm Repository
Nez Perce bean	*Phaseolus vulgaris*	Salt Spring Seeds, Grass Root Seeds
Nootka rose	*Rosa nutkana*	Forestfarm Nursery, Methow Native Nursery, Landscape Alaska, Gardens North
Nootka rose garlic	*Allium sativum* var. *sativum*	Territorial Seed Company
Northwestern greenling apple	*Malus X domestica*	Weston's Antique Apples
Olympia oyster	*Ostrea lurida*	Taylor Shellfish Farms, Inc., Little Skookum Shellfish Growers
Olympic blackberry	*Rubus ursinus X*	El Nativo Growers, Inc., Wallace W. Hansen Native Plants of the Northwest Native Plant Nursery & Gardens
Orcas pear	*Pyrus communis*	Raintree Nursery, One Green World
Oregon champion gooseberry	*Ribes divaricatum*	Wallace W. Hansen Native Plants of the Northwest Native Plant Nursery & Gardens
Oregon delicious melon	*Cucumis melo*	Seeds of Diversity
Oregon giant bean	*Phaseolus vulgaris*	Seeds of Change, Prairie Garden Seeds
Orenco apple	*Malus X domestica*	Greenmantle Nursery
Oval-leaved or Gray blueberry	*Vaccinium ovalifolium*	One Green World
Ozette potato	*Solanum tuberosum*	Seed Savers Exchange, Milk Ranch Specialty Potatoes
Pacific crabapple or Swamp crabapple	*Malus fusca*	Burnt Ridge Nursery, Streamside Native Plants
Pacific razor clam	*Siliqua patula*	Quinault Pride Seafood
Pale serviceberry	*Amelanchier pallida*	Wallace W. Hansen Native Plants of the Northwest Native Plant Nursery & Gardens
Prickly rose	*Rosa acicularis*	Gardens North, Greenmantle Nursery

COMMON NAME	SCIENTIFIC NAME	SUPPLIERS
Quilcenes oyster	*Crassostrea gigas*	Taylor Shellfish Farms, Inc., Coast Seafoods Company
Red huckleberry or Deciduous huckleberry	*Vaccinium parvifolium*	Forestfarm Nursery, Burnt Ridge Nursery, Streamside Native Plants
Red-osier dogwood	*Cornus sericea*	Nature Hills Nursery, Inc., Methow Native Nursery
Rosehips, from Dwarf	*Rosa gymnocarpa*	Streamside Native Plants
Salal	*Gaultheria shallon*	Larner Seeds, One Green World, Streamside Native Plants
Salmonberry	*Rubus spectabilis*	Forestfarm Nursery, One Green World, Streamside Native Plants
Saskatoon berry	*Amelanchier alnifolia*	Forestfarm Nursery, Burnt Ridge Nursery, Methow Native Nursery
Scallop	*Argopecten, Chlamys, Crassadoma,* and *Patinopecten* species	Little Skookum Shellfish Growers, Qutekcak Shellfish Hatchery
Sea urchin	*Strongylocentrotus* species	The Lobster Man
Seaside strawberry	*Fragaria chiloensis*	Burnt Ridge Nursery, Streamside Native Plants
Sitka mountain-ash	*Sorbus sitchensis*	Burnt Ridge Nursery
Snow Creek oyster	*Crassostrea gigas*	Taylor Shellfish Farms, Inc.
Soft-shell clam or Soft-shell mussel	*Mya arenaria*	Coast Seafoods Company, Taylor Shellfish, Whiskey Creek Shellfish, Lummi Hatchery
Soopolallie, Russet, or Cascade buffalo-berry	*Shepherdia canadensis*	Streamside Native Plants
Spokane beauty apple	*Malus X domestica*	Kiyokawa Family Orchards
Sticky or Pioneer gooseberry	*Ribes lobbii*	Streamside Native Plants
Swamp rose	*Rosa pisocarpa*	Streamside Native Plants
Tall Oregon grape	*Mahonia aquifolium*	Forestfarm Nursery, Methow Native Nursery, Streamside Native Plants
Thimbleberry	*Rubus parviflorus*	Forestfarm Nursery, One Green World, Streamside Native Plants
Trailing wild blackberry	*Rubus ursinus*	El Nativo Growers, Inc.
Umpqua Flats oyster	*Crassostrea gigas*	Umpqua Aquaculture
Wenatchee Moorpark apricot	*Prunus armeniaca*	Nature Hills Nursery, Inc., C&O Nursery
Wild raspberry	*Rubus idaeus*	One Green World, Methow Native Nursery
Wood's rose	*Rosa woodsii*	Methow Native Nursery
Yaquina oyster	*Crassostrea gigas*	Taylor Shellfish Farms, Inc., Oregon Oyster Farms, Inc.

Abundant Life Seeds
P.O. Box 157
Saginaw, OR 97472
(541) 767-9606
als@abundantlifeseeds.com
www.abundantlifeseeds.com

Alutiiq Pride Shellfish Hatchery
P.O. Box 369
Seward, AK 99664
(907) 224-5181
hatchery@crrcalaska.org

Anacortes Aquaculture, LLC
4305 Kingsway
Anacortes, WA 98221-3287
(360) 299-2530
cih_csp@hotmail.com

Brenner Oyster Co.
402 S. 333rd St., Suite 102
Federal Way, WA 98003
(253) 929-1562
bbrenbun@aol.com
www.jjbrenner.com

Burnt Ridge Nursery & Orchards, Inc.
432 Burnt Ridge Road
Onalaska, WA 98570
(360) 985-2873
mail@burntridgenursery.com
www.burntridgenursery.com

Callahan Seeds
P.O. Box 5531
Central Point, OR 97502
(541) 855-1164

C&O Nursery
P.O. Box 116
Wenatchee, WA 98807-0116
(509) 662-7164
www.c-onursery.com

Coast Seafoods Company
14711 NE 29th Place, Suite 111
Bellevue, WA 98007
(425) 702-8800
info@coastseafoods.com
www.coastseafoods.com

Danamac Acres
P.O. Box 4542
Mile 1/4 Farm Loop Road
Palmer, AK 99645
(907) 745-2583
mncscott@ak.net

El Nativo Growers, Inc.
200 S. Peckham Road
Azusa, CA 91702
(626) 969-8449
sales@elnativogrowers.com
www.elnativogrowers.com

Forestfarm Nursery
990 Tetherow Road
Williams, OR 97544
(541) 846-7269
plants@forestfarm.com
www.forestfarm.com

Freshwater Farms
5851 Myrtle Avenue
Eureka, CA 95503
(707) 444-8261, (800) 200-8969
www.freshwaterfarms.com

Fritz Creek Gardens
P.O. Box 15226
Homer, AK 99603
(907) 235-4969
www.alaskahardy.com

Fruit-tree.com Nursery
(503) 628-0910
info@fruit-tree.com
www.fruit-tree.com

Gardens North
5984 Third Line Road
North Gower, ON KOA 2T0
Canada
(613) 489-0065
seed@gardensnorth.com
www.gardensnorth.com

Grass Root Seeds
Box #397
Princeton, BC V0X 1W0
Canada
(250) 295-5477
www.grassroot-seeds.com

Greenmantle Nursery
3010 Ettersburg Road
Garberville, CA 95542
(707) 986-7504
www.greenmantlenursery.com

Hama Hama Oyster Company
P.O. Box 250
Lilliwaup, WA 98555
(360) 877-5811
www.hamahamaoysters.com

J. L. Hudson, Seedsman
Star Route 2, Box 337
La Honda, CA 94020-9733
inquiry@jlhudsonseeds.net
www.jlhudsonseeds.net

Joseph D. Postman Plant Pathologist
USDA/Agricultural Research Service
National Clonal Germplasm Repository
33447 Peoria Road
Corvallis, OR 97330
(541) 738-4220
postmanj@bcc.orst.edu
www.ars.usda.gov

Kenaitze Greenhouse & Gardens
P.O. Box 988
255 N. Ames
Kenai, AK 99611
(907) 283-3633
lobelia58@hotmail.com

Kiyokawa Family Orchards
8129 Clear Creek Road
Parkdale, OR 97041
(541) 352-7115
www.mthoodfruit.com

Landscape Alaska
P.O. Box 32654
Juneau, AK 99803
(907) 790-4916
www.landscapealaska.com

Larner Seeds
P.O. Box 407
Bolinas, CA 94924
(415) 868-9407
info@larnerseeds.com
www.learnerseeds.com

Little Skookum Shellfish Growers
P.O. Box 1157
Shelton, WA 98584
(360) 426-9759
www.skookumshellfish.com

Lummi Shellfish Hatchery
2616 Kwina Road
Bellingham, WA 98226
(360) 384-2303
shellops@memes.com
www.lummi-nsn.org

Maine Organic Farmers and Gardeners Association
P.O. Box 170
257 Crosby Brook Road
Unity, ME 04988
(207) 568-4142
mofga@mofga.org
www.mofga.org

Methow Native Nursery
19 Aspen Lane
Winthrop, WA 98862
(509) 996-3562
methownatives@methownet.com
www.methownatives.com

Milk Ranch Specialty Potatoes, LLC
20094 Highway 149
Powderhorn, CO 81243
(970) 641-5634
www.milkranch.com

Native Plants of the Northwest Native Plant Nursery & Gardens
2158 Bower Ct S.E.
(503) 581-2638
Salem, OR 97301
www.nwplants.com

Nature Hills Nursery, Inc.
3334 North 88th Plaza
Omaha, NE 68134
(402) 934-8116
www.naturehills.com

One Green World
28696 S. Cramer Road
Molalla, OR 97038-8576
(877) 353-4028, (503) 651-3005
www.onegreenworld.com

Oregon Exotics Rare Fruit Nursery
1065 Messinger Road
Grants Pass, OR 97527-9408
(541) 846-7578
www.exoticfruit.com

Oregon Oyster Farms, Inc.
6878 Yaquina Bay Road
Newport, OR 97365
(541) 265-5078
www.oregonoyster.com

Pacific Rim Native Plant Nursery
P.O. Box 413
Chilliwack, BC V2P 6J7
Canada
plants@hillkeep.ca
www.hillkeep.ca

Prairie Garden Seeds
Box 118
Cochin, SK S0M 0L0
Canada
(306) 386-2737
prairie.seeds@sasktel.net
www.prseeds.ca

Quinault Pride Seafood
P.O. Box 217
Taholah, WA 98587
(360) 276-4431
gensly@quinault.org
http://209.206.175.158

Qutekcak Shellfish Hatchery
P.O. Box 369
Seward, AK 99664
(907) 224-5181
qshatch@arctic.net

Raintree Nursery
391 Butts Rd.
Morton, WA 98356
(360) 496-6400
www.raintreenursery.com

Salt Spring Seeds
Box 444, Ganges P.O.
Salt Spring Island, BC V8K 2W1
Canada
(250) 537-5269
www.saltspringseeds.com
www.seedsanctuary.com

Seed Savers Exchange
3094 North Winn Road
Decorah, IA 52101
(563) 382-5990
www.seedsavers.org

Seeds of Change
(888) 762-7333
www.seedsofchange.com

Seeds of Diversity Canada
P.O. Box 36, Stn Q
Toronto, ON M4T 2L7
Canada
(866) 509-7333
mail@seeds.ca
www.seeds.ca

Seeds Trust
P.O. Box 4619
Ketchum, ID 83340
(208) 788-4363
support3@seedsave.org
www.seedsave.org

Streamside Native Plants: Division of Viking Marine/Outdoors Ltd.
RR #1, Site 160, Comp 27
Bowser, BC V0R 1G0
Canada
(250) 338-7509
Richard@streamsidenativeplants.com
http://members.shaw.ca/nativeplants/
streamside_home.html

The Lobster Man
1807 Mast Tower Road
Vancouver, BC V6H 3X7
Canada
(604) 687-4531
info@lobsterman.com
www.lobsterman.com

The Territorial Seed Company
P.O. Box 158
Cottage Grove, OR 97424-0061
(800) 626-0866
www.territorial-seed.com

Trees of Antiquity
20 Wellsona Road
Paso Robles, CA 93446
(805) 467-9909
www.treesofantiquity.com

Umpqua Aquaculture, Inc.
Cindy Sardina and Vern Simmons
723 Ork Rock Road
P.O. Box 1287
Winchester Bay, OR 97467
(541) 271-5684
umpquaaqua@harborside.com
www.umpquaoysters.com

U.S. Abalone
245 Davenport Landing Road
P.O. Box 254
Davenport, CA 95017
(831) 457-2700
mail@usabalone.com
www.usabalone.com

Weeks Berry Nursery
6494 Windsor Island Road
Keizer, OR 97303
(503) 393-8112
www.weeksberry.com

Weston Antique Apples
5470 S. Overlook Drive
New Berlin, WI 53146
(262) 679-2862
www.westonapples.com

Whiskey Creek Shellfish Hatchery
2975 Netarts Bay Drive
Tillamook, OR 97141-8330
(503) 815-8323

PHOTOGRAPHY

We extend our special thanks to all who contributed photos to this publication.

Larry Allain, USGS: Sitka mountain-ash ❧ Robyn P. Angliss, National Marine Mammal Laboratory, NOAA: beluga whale ❧ George Barron: bear's head, lobster mushroom ❧ Mike Bender, USFWS: black bear ❧ Br. Alfred Brousseau, Saint Mary's College: white chanterelle, bird cherry ❧ Captain Budd Christman, NOAA: woodland caribou, spotted seal, Steller's sea lion, walrus ❧ David Cowles: Dungeness crab, butter clam, heart cockle, horse clam, octopus, introduced "Japanese" oyster ❧ Kelly Curtis: Pacific razor clam ❧ Lyrae Emerson, BSc Environmental Sciences: Pacific crabapple ❧ Gulf of the Farallones National Marine Sanctuary: sea urchin ❧ Bob Glanzman, The Puget Sound Kiwi Co.: Gillette fig ❧ Steve Hillebrand, USFWS: black-tailed deer ❧ Dave Ingram: coastal black gooseberry ❧ Louis M. Landry: fiddlehead fern ❧ Greene Lawson: chanterelle ❧ Virginia Maffitt: bitterroot ❧ Hunt McLean, Yelm Earth Worm and Castings Farm: Lorz Italian garlic ❧ National Oceanic and Atmospheric Administration (NOAA): giant kelp, gray whale ❧ Jon R. Nickles, USFWS: Dall sheep ❧ OAR/National Undersea Research Program (NURP); Alaska Department of Fish and Game: lingcod, yelloweye rockfish ❧ One Green World: Hudson's golden gem apple, Charlotte peach ❧ Oregon Department of Fish and Wildlife (ODFW): cabezon, petrale ❧ Pacific Northwest National Laboratory: chinook salmon ❧ Raintree Nursery: Orcas pear ❧ Jim Riley: bunchberry ❧ Seed Savers Exchange (SSE): Ozette potato ❧ Linda Snook, CBNMS: bocaccio ❧ Dane Springmeyer: blue camas ❧ Robert D. and Nancy J. Turner: cottonwood mushroom, pine mushroom, eelgrass, balsamroot, biscuitroot, cow parsnip, Hooker's onion, mountain potato, northern riceroot, springbank clover, wapato, yampa, yellow glacier lilly, cloudberry, blackcap raspberry, salmonberry, Cascade bilberry, Canada blueberry, evergreen huckleberry, red huckleberry, highbush cranberry, beaked hazelnut, gray currant, Wood's rose, salal, creeping snowberry, soopolallie ❧ Underwater Harvesters Association: geoduck ❧ USDA-NRCS PLANTS Database: Cascade Oregon grape ❧ Dana Visalli: Olympic blackberry, licorice fern, chocolate lily, pink slipper orchid, dwarf mountain blueberry, choke cherry, seaside strawberry, Cascade moose, mountain goat ❧ Scott Vlaun, courtesy of Seeds of Change: Oregon giant bean, Hooker's Sweet Indian corn, Inchelium red garlic ❧ Margaret Williams, © Nevada Native Plant Society: lingonberry ❧ Matthew Whiting, WSU: bing cherry ❧ Michael Wilhelm: coho salmon, sockeye salmon

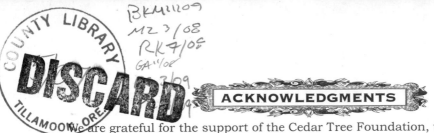

ACKNOWLEDGMENTS

We are grateful for the support of the Cedar Tree Foundation, the Lillian Goldman Charitable Trust, and the Haury Fund. Debra Sohm Lawson of Ecotrust graciously hosted the Portland workshop, and along with Elizabeth Woody, Craig Jacobson, and Spencer Beebe, offered means to integrate this effort into the larger food systems and indigenous leadership work being done on behalf of Salmon Nation. The following organizations participated in this effort: Ecotrust, Chefs Collaborative, Slow Food, Institute for Culture and Ecology, Wild Food Adventures, University of Washington, Evergreen College, Organic Seed Alliance, Inn at Cave B, University of British Columbia, Sooke Harbour House, Quillascut Farm School, Bon Appétit, and the Indigenous Caucus of the Society for Ecological Restoration.

We owe a great debt to the following field workers and scholars whose published works we have built upon: Nancy Turner, Fernando and Marlene Divina, Louis Drue, Rae Hopkins, Frank Lake, Kathy Mendelson, Erna Gunther, Richard Nelson, John Kallas, Eugene Hunn, Dennis Martinez, Adam Szczawinski, Harriet Kuhnlein, David French, Edward C. Wolf, Seth Zuckerman, and M. Kat Anderson. We owe even a larger debt to all First Nations of Salmon Nation.

For design and production, we thank Howard Silverman, Andrew Fuller, and Jennifer Marlow at Ecotrust.

CONTACTS

American Livestock Breeds Conservancy
www.albc-usa.org
Don Bixby, dbixby@albc-usa.org

Chefs Collaborative
www.chefscollaborative.org
Jennifer Hall, jennifer@chefscollaborative.org

Cultural Conservancy
www.nativeland.org
Melissa Nelson, mknelson@lgc.org

Ecotrust
www.ecotrust.org
Debra Sohm Lawson, dsohm@ecotrust.org
Elizabeth Woody, liz@ecotrust.org

Native Seeds/SEARCH
www.nativeseeds.org
Kevin Dahl, kdahl@nativeseeds.org

Center for Sustainable Environments
www.environment.nau.edu
Gary Paul Nabhan, Gary.Nabhan@nau.edu

Seed Savers Exchange
www.seedsavers.org
Kent Whealy, kent@seedsavers.org

Slow Food Canada
www.slowfood.ca
Sinclair Philip, sinclair@sookeharbourhouse.com

Slow Food USA
www.slowfoodusa.org
Makalé Faber, makale@slowfoodusa.org